THE RIGHT WAY TO DO WRONG

HARRY HOUDINI (1874–1926) was born Erik Weisz in Budapest, Hungary, the son of a rabbi. The family moved to Appleton, Wisconsin, when he was four, and changed their name from Weisz to Weiss, and Erik to Ehrich. To help support the family, Houdini first performed on stage in a trapeze act at the age of nine. After moving to New York at age 12, he became interested in magic, and concocted a stage name: 'Harry' was an Americanized version of his nickname, Ehrie, and 'Houdini' was inspired by magician Robert Houdin. Houdini's big break came in 1899 when he was offered a contract to perform on the best vaudeville stages in the US. Now known as the "Handcuff King," Houdini toured Europe for five years, and upon returning to the U.S. began to perform the death-defying stunts that would make him one of the most famous people in the world, and one of the most popular early movie stars. He published *The Right Way to Do Wrong* in 1906 and edited *Conjurers' Monthly Magazine* in 1906–7. Towards the end of his life he famously dedicated himself to debunking spiritualists, even having an intense public feud with spiritualist-believer Arthur Conan Doyle. In 1926, after a performance in Montreal, an admirer visiting him backstage punched an unprepared Houdini in the stomach to test his famous muscle control. Houdini's appendix ruptured and, after peritonitis set in, he died—after one last performance in Detroit—at age 52.

TELLER has been the quieter half of magic duo Penn & Teller since 1975. He has written five books and enjoyed successful runs on Broadway, sold-out world tours, starring roles in TV series, and the longest-running headline act in Las Vegas. He is an Emmy, Writers Guild Award, Obie and Drama Critics Circle winner.

THE NEVERSINK LIBRARY

I was by no means the only reader of books on board the Neversink. *Several other sailors were diligent readers, though their studies did not lie in the way of belles-lettres. Their favourite authors were such as you may find at the book-stalls around Fulton Market; they were slightly physiological in their nature. My book experiences on board of the frigate proved an example of a fact which every book-lover must have experienced before me, namely, that though public libraries have an imposing air, and doubtless contain invaluable volumes, yet, somehow, the books that prove most agreeable, grateful, and companionable, are those we pick up by chance here and there; those which seem put into our hands by Providence; those which pretend to little, but abound in much.* —HERMAN MELVILLE, *WHITE JACKET*

THE RIGHT WAY
TO DO WRONG
A UNIQUE SELECTION OF WRITINGS BY
HISTORY'S GREATEST ESCAPE ARTIST

HARRY HOUDINI

INTRODUCTION BY TELLER

MELVILLE HOUSE PUBLISHING
BROOKLYN · LONDON

THE RIGHT WAY TO DO WRONG

Harry Houdini published the first edition of *The Right Way to Do Wrong* in 1906. This Melville House edition compiles the best of that book with pieces from *Conjurers' Monthly Magazine*, a magazine edited by Houdini between 1906 and 1907; chapters from *Magical Rope Ties and Escapes*, 1920; and chapters from *Miracle Mongers and Their Methods*, 1920.

This edition © Melville House 2012
Introduction © Teller, 2012

Design by Christopher King

First Melville House printing: September 2012

Melville House Publishing
145 Plymouth Street
Brooklyn, NY 11201

www.mhpbooks.com

ISBN: 978-1-61219-166-9

Manufactured in the United States of America
1 2 3 4 5 6 7 8 9 10

     Library of Congress Cataloging-in-Publication Data
Houdini, Harry, 1874-1926.
 The right way to do wrong / Harry Houdini.
     p. cm.
 ISBN 978-1-61219-166-9
1. Criminology. 2. Swindlers and swindling. I. Title.
HV6251.H6 2012
364.16'3--dc23
                         2012029424

CONTENTS

INTRODUCTION

BY TELLER

Houdini knew marketing. He called himself "The Great Self-Liberator, World's Handcuff King, and Prison-Breaker." That was the brand he hammered home to the public as he built his career. And it stuck.

When we think of Houdini, we picture a defiant little muscle man with penetrating blue eyes; we see a prisoner naked except for manacles bundled in front of his crotch; baffled police returning to a prison cell from which Houdini has inexplicably vanished; a handcuffed mad-man stripped to shorts and plummeting from a bridge to certain death in a river; a human sacrifice, straitjacketed, hanging by his ankles upside down over a mobbed metropolitan street as he writhes and thrashes, rips himself free, then drops the straitjacket into the sea of upturned faces and extends his arms for applause like an inverted Jesus.

But as with any good brand, the image oversimplifies the product. The public's invulnerable jock superhero had an intellectual side. One Houdini autograph reads, "My brain is the key that sets me free." Houdini revered learning (his father was a rabbi) and was pained by his limited education (he went to school only till the sixth grade).

But Houdini made a specialty of steamrolling obstacles. As he built his career, he invested most of his fortune in books. His collection filled his home from basement to attic. He employed a librarian and once boasted to a correspondent, "You know, I actually live in a library." When he died in 1926, his books were valued at half a million dollars, the equivalent of more than $6 million today. A portion of Houdini's collection is one of the treasures of the Library of Congress.

Houdini also aspired to be a writer. His expertise was in deception, both legitimate (magic) and illegitimate (crime), and he turned out fascinating books, pamphlets, and newspaper articles. You are about to read some of his liveliest and least known writings.

You'll notice two contrasting voices in Houdini's style. One is brash and sounds like a tough little street-fighter. That's raw Houdini, the sixth-grade-educated self-made man braying out his very definite views. The other style is all curlicued and upholstered, with ten-dollar Latinate words, complex sentences, and quotations from classical literature. The content is Houdini's, but translated from sideshow to lecture hall by ghostwriters who made him sound like the literate individual his rabbi father might have admired.

In the raw Houdini category, we've unearthed choice selections from *Conjurers' Monthly Magazine*, a trade journal Houdini put out filled with news, history, and advice for brother magicians. Here he talks nuts and bolts about magical performance. Houdini worked in an age before electronic amplification, when stage stars needed voices like opera singers. Houdini teaches you how you, too, can launch your consonants to the cheap seats.

Magic in Houdini's day was no better than it is now, and Houdini's not afraid to say so. Most performers go from trick to trick and "content themselves with mere doing," as Houdini bluntly puts it. Houdini, who had seen and known the greats of magic, offers alternatives.

You also get to meet the brawler Houdini, the braggart alpha male who tolerated no imitators and who would rip into the competition like a fighting cock. You may find Houdini's ranting against copyists a bit grating, but it's easy to understand his rage. Magic is a niche form of showbiz. Magicians don't enjoy systematic protections for their original work, the way, say, musicians do. If you compose a song and somebody else records it, that person owes you credit and royalties. But magicians like Houdini put years into developing material that muttonheads ripped off overnight. It pissed him off. So I'm not surprised that Houdini is scrappy on that point.

Magicians fool their audiences. But only for a little while, only in the theater. After the curtain call, you may wonder how the magician seemed to produce a ghost, but you don't believe the show proved ghosts are real. You have been mystified, not suckered. This distinction was a moral point for Houdini, and much of his writing was devoted to exposing people who were passing off tricks as reality.

At the end of the 1900s, big American cities were getting bigger and more anonymous, and the class of urban stealth-criminals grew: burglars, pickpockets, shoplifters, and confidence operators, who depended more on guile than brute force. Houdini was in a good position to get the inside dope on such operations. For the sake of his publicity-stunt jailbreaks, he cultivated warm relationships with police all over the US and Europe, and his police friends let him interview criminals. They were flattered by the attention of the most famous stage performer in the world, and proudly spilled their methods. Houdini recounts the most amusing and thought provoking of those confessions in *The Right Way to do Wrong*, from which we present choice selections. It's always struck me as a blueprint for a great television series.

Why do we care so much about crime in a world as secure as the one you and I live in? As Houdini explains, understanding skullduggery helps protect us from becoming victims. But I think there's a sunnier reason: we lead safe, well-fed lives, and the animal part of our nature hasn't grasped that yet. Part of us still hungers to chase our steak through the forest and kill it with our own sharp teeth. So the people who love to read about crime and violence are generally gentle folk like you and me. We watch forensic dissections on TV while we enjoy our dinner, and that's just as it should be. In *The Right Way To Do Wrong* my favorite scam is the one in the jewelry store with the chewing gum. Watch for it.

Just southeast of Houdini's interest in crooks is his love of the disgusting and sensational sideshow arts like stone-eating and beer-spouting, which he wrote about in *Miracle Mongers and their Methods*. I do not recommend pursuing a new career based on Houdini's colorful instructions in these wonders. Remember, a magician's art is to make dull reality look like fascinating impossibility. Houdini called this "mystification," and added with balls the size of Gibraltar, "but I do tricks that *nobody* can find out."

So as you read, whether it's the rough or the refined

Houdini, please remember that though you love him (and you will) he was a showman, a brand-builder, not a historian. Tacitus, the ancient Roman writer of histories—and before you decide this paragraph was written by a ghostwriter, I admit I once taught high-school Latin—said "*Fingunt simul creduntque*," "They make it up, and at the same time, they believe it." That's frequently true of Houdini. It's inevitably true of anyone who builds a brand. It's certainly true of me as I write this. And if you listen to yourself tell the stories that make life worthwhile, you'll probably find it's true of you, too.

THE RIGHT WAY TO DO WRONG

HELPFUL HINTS FOR YOUNG MAGICIANS UNDER EIGHTY

IN WINNING YOUR AUDIENCE, REMEMBER THAT "Manners make fortunes," so don't be impertinent.

An old trick well done is far better than a new trick with no effect.

Never tell the audience how good you are; they will soon find that out for themselves.

Nothing can give greater delight to the gentler sex than to have some flowers handed to them that you have produced from a hat or paper cone.

Rabbit tricks are positive successes.

Never work to fool a magician; always work to your audience. You may think your trick is old, but it is always new to members of your audience.

An old trick in a new dress is always a pleasant change.

When practicing a new trick, try it in front of a looking glass, accompanying your moves with your entire patter.

Don't drag your tricks, but work as quickly as you can, bearing in mind the Latin proverb, "Make haste slowly."

When your audience is far distant from you, pantomime work will be well appreciated.

Well-chosen remarks on topics of the day are always in order.

The newspapers generally commented more on Heller's wit than on his magic.

Always have a short sentence ready in case a trick should go wrong. One magician, who has the misfortune to blunder often, says, "Ladies and gentlemen, mistakes will happen, and that is one of them."

Walk right out on stage, and tell your tale to your audience, and perhaps many will believe it.

It is far more difficult to give a trial show to a house full of seats and one manager than to a packed house and no manager.

ADDRESSING AN AUDIENCE

THE GREAT TROUBLE WITH MAGICIANS IS THE fact that they believe when they have bought a certain trick or piece of apparatus, and know the method of procedure, that they are full-fledged mystifiers. The fact really is, it is not the trick itself, neither is it the mere handling of it, but a successful presentation depends on the address in connection with the presentation. It is historically recorded that Demosthenes, having an impediment in his speech, placed pebbles in his mouth and spoke to the rolling waves. During nearly all my lifetime I have had occasion to address large audiences, and a pertinent fact comes to mind. In October, 1900, at the Berlin Winter Garden, which is really a type of railroad station, I was the only one who could be heard all over the house. At the New York Hippodrome, where I performed for two consecutive seasons, my voice carried to all parts of that vast audience. As a matter of fact, I was told that I could be heard out in the lobby. The acoustic properties were wonderful in the Hippodrome, but there is something about a man's personality that is lost when in a huge place; just as the man who is accustomed to speaking in a small circle is lost when he gets on the stage and vice versa. I have no objections to giving magicians the secret of my manner of address and what I regard is the right speaking voice.

Incidentally, once upon a time, my grammar was corrected by a newspaper man. It was on my first trip on the Orpheum Circuit, and strange to say, our beloved Dean, Harry Kellar, had a similar experience. Allan Dale in one of his criticisms corrected him in the same manner. Mr. Kellar's remark was: "When I done this trick," etc. In the criticism, Allan Dale said, "I did, Mr. Kellar, I did, Mr. Kellar, I did, Mr. Kellar." Kellar informed me that he took the hint and went under training. I do not believe that Allan Dale knows to this day how grateful Kellar was for the criticism. When an artist, even a magician, is corrected by a critic, he should not be dismayed nor look upon it as wasted. He should consider it a friendly favor and look upon it the same as I have always looked upon criticism. Constructive criticism is wonderfully helpful. Imagine having a great big newspaper man watch the performance and then write a criticism free of charge. Why, it is a wonderfully beneficial thing as I look at it.

If you were to engage a critic to correct your performance he would charge hundreds of dollars; so, instead of letting the criticism go to waste, or becoming antagonistic, the newspaperman's correction of your performance should be gratefully accepted. When I had an engagement at an extensive place where I was afraid my voice would not carry, I would actually go in training for that place. I would run around the block in the morning at a dogtrot and get my lungs in good condition, for it is a fact that in my work I require wonderful lungs to use in my physical manifestations before an audience. I would also take long walks, away from habitation and address an imaginary audience. I remember in Moscow, Russia, 1903, I went to the racetrack and delivered my speech to my imaginary audience with all the gestures, and in the course of my remarks I said, "I defy the police departments of the world to hold me. I challenge any police official to handcuff me." And strange as it may appear, one of the spy detectives, or secret policemen, overheard me. In about twenty minutes, as I was roaming around the race track, I was surrounded by policemen, thinking that I was a mad man, and when I gave them an explanation they just roared with laughter. Thereupon, I used them as my audience and they made corrections regarding my speech, for which I was thankful. In 1900, on my first trip to England, I had the good fortune to meet quite a number of the legitimate stars.

Among others I met Herman Vezin, the understudy of Sir Henry Irving. I was, at that time, called "The Syllable Accenting American," because I would spell my words, figuratively, that they should be carried to the gallery. I never spoke to the first row. My method of addressing an audience, as a result of experience, was as follows: I would walk down to the footlights, actually put one foot over the electric globes as if I were going to spring among the people, and then hurl my voice, saying "Ladies and gentlemen." I was told by a number of men that in the Boston Polyclinic and various other schools they would illustrate my method, and then the class would go to Keith's Theatre to hear my enunciation and manner of delivery.

When you can make the men in the gallery hear each syllable, the audience in front, or downstairs, are also most effectually served. When you introduce an experiment, apply yourself seriously. Don't think because you perform a trick well, or the apparatus is detection-proof from the viewpoint of an ordinary audience, that you have conquered the world of mystery, and that you reign supreme. Work with determination that you intend to make them believe what you say. Say it as if you mean it and believe it yourself. If you believe your own claim to miracle doing and are sincere in your work, you are bound to succeed. The reasons magicians do not forge to the front more than they do now, is because they are content themselves with a mere doing, and imagine they have the act complete; that all they have to do is lay the apparatus on the table and go from one trick to the other. The experiment and apparatus are both of secondary consideration. Your determination to improve the seriousness of your endeavors means success, and if you are a natural comedian (I do not mean a buffoon, or something which does not become your personality) you may easily inject a tinge of humor in your work. But do not strain that point; it should come naturally and with ease, or be left alone. Herrmann's method with an audience was: As soon as he appeared to their gaze, he bowed and smiled all the way to the footlights, as if he were tickled to death to have the honor of appearing before them, and the effect on his audience was salutatory and he won their sympathy forthwith. Dean Kellar's method was to walk in just the same as he would into a house party, welcoming all. He knew he was presenting a line of feats that the majority might have known, but he handled each number beautifully and he knew that the audience loved to see him do it. Therefore, everything he presented inspired the audience to a feeling of kindliness and likeableness to him in appreciation of his work. If you want to be a success, make up your mind that your address to the audience will be the most important item of your performance.

THE FRENCH LETTER CUFF

Houdini explains "one of the most interesting contests that ever fell to his lot," an episode involving a handcuff performer named Kleppini in June 1902. French Letter handcuffs open when the correct word is entered in their mechanism.

WE WERE TOURING HOLLAND, WHEN A FRIEND sent me a bill and newspaper clipping, announcing in huge, fat type that Kleppini was about to appear at Circus Sidoli, in Dortmund, Germany, after returning from Holland, where he had defeated the American, Houdini, at his own game. Kleppini further claimed that I had handcuffed him, only to see him escape, while I had met with defeat when handcuffed by him.

This was more than pride could endure. I had a heated argument with my Herr Director, Althoff, who at first refused to allow me to follow up Kleppini and force him to retract; but when I said it was leave of absence or quit for good, he yielded, granted me five days' leave, and I left at once for Dortmund.

Arriving at Essen, a few miles distant from Dortmund, and a town where I had many good friends, I first visited a barber and had him glue a false moustache on my lip, and so fix my hair that I looked like an old man. Then with my small grip filled with "handcuff-king-defeaters," I was off to Dortmund and the circus, where I found the attendance very light. Kleppini appeared, making his speech in which he claimed to have defeated me. Instantly I was on my feet, crying "*Nicht wahr*," meaning "Not true." He asked how I knew this, and I said I was in the know, whereupon he finally offered to wager that he was right. With that I took a flying leap of twenty-two feet downwards to the centre of the ring or *menage*, as it is called in Germany, and cried, "You say I am not telling the truth. Well, look! I am Houdini!"

During the controversy that followed I told Kleppini and his manager what honest folk thought of performers and managers who employed misleading and untruthful advertising matter; and I offered 5000 marks if Kleppini would let me handcuff him. Also I offered to escape from his Chinese pillory. He tried to evade the issue, saying he would look me up later, but I insisted that he deposit the money before he started, as I had mine with me.

Herr Director Sidoli refused to make good his advertisements and to back Kleppini for the sum mentioned, so I returned to my seat, and the audience left the circus building in droves, disgusted by the misrepresentations.

The next morning, June 18, Herr Reutter, business manager of the circus, came to my hotel with a proposition that I should engage myself one night for a duel with Kleppini, which I refused. Herr Reutter then asked me whether I would handcuff Kleppini if the latter challenged me, and I replied that this I would certainly do. So he begged me to remain one day longer, not allowing anyone to know of my presence in town, however. As I had been working steadily since leaving New York, I was in sad need of rest, so I waited all day in my room, having all meals sent to me. On the morning of June 19 I arose with the lark—to face huge bills announcing: "Houdini challenged and will appear at the Circus Ceasur Sidoli this evening. Kleppini will allow himself to be hand-cuffed and will immediately free himself."

I was more amused than angry. I simply polished my various handcuffs, oiled the mechanism and waited.

Kleppini sent for me. I refused to go to him. He called at the hotel. I would not receive him. Manager Reutter then came to me and asked me what cuffs I intended to lock on his star. I said he was at liberty to choose the cuff to be used, and pointed to the twelve cuffs laid out for his inspection.

There was one pair of French letter cuffs that caught his fancy, and I permitted him to examine them closely. Reutter then inquired in a peculiar tone, as if feigning indifference: "What letters or word opens this cuff?"

I perceived his trick at once, and securing his promise that he would not tell Kleppini, I replied, "Clefs," which means keys. At the same time I showed him just how to work them. He fell into the trap, and asked me whether he might take these cuffs for Herr Director Sidoli to examine them before the performance, and I told him he was quite at liberty to do so, provided they were not shown to Kleppini. This promise also was given, and he departed, keeping the cuffs in his possession four hours. Of course I knew that during this time Kleppini was fa-miliarizing himself with the cuffs, but I still had a trick up my own sleeve.

That night at the circus I occupied a box seat, and

when Kleppini threw out his daring challenge, I entered the ring with my bag of cuffs. I said that I had no objection to his advertising his willingness to let me handcuff him, but I did object to his stating he could get out until he had made good. The audience was with me, and I told him to take his choice of the twelve cuffs.

As I anticipated, he sprang like a tiger on the French letter cuff. He had taken them closed, and ran with feverish haste into his cabinet.

He remained within about three minutes, whereupon I cried: "Ladies and gentlemen, do not let him tell you that the cuffs have been locked. They are open. He will return and say he opened them."

This brought him out of his cabinet waving the cuffs like a crazy man, and crying, "I will open these cuffs. I challenge Houdini to lock them on me. I'll show him that it is us Germans who lead the world."

As he had tried the cuffs in the cabinet, he was positive that he could beat them. And I was just as positive that the opposite conditions would prevail.

He now started to goad me into locking them on quickly, pressing me all over the circus. So violent were my efforts, that my heart beat like a trip hammer, and my face turned pale from exertion. From this Kleppini gathered that I thought myself even then defeated. So he walked to the center of the ring, with the handcuffs locked upon him, and cried: "After I open these handcuffs, I will allow Madame Kleppini to open them. She is very clever in this branch of work, and she will open them in five seconds."

I smiled grimly and took the floor. "Ladies and gentlemen, you can all go home. I do not lock a cuff on a man merely to let him escape. If he tries this cuff until doomsday, he cannot open it. To prove this, though the regular closing time of the circus is 10.30, I will allow him to remain here until 2.30."

He went into his cabinet at nine o'clock. When the big ballet feature came on at 9.30, he was not ready. At 11, almost the entire audience had gone, and Kleppini was still in his cabinet. Herr Director Sidoli became enraged, and instructed his servants to "out with Kleppini," and they lifted the cabinet up bodily and threw it over. Kleppini ran like a hunted animal into the manager's dressing room. The rest of the show might have gone on, but the audience rose as a man and went out.

At midnight, by which time I had left my place in the box, and was standing guard over the dressing-room door, I permitted Madame Kleppini to join her husband, at his request. About one o'clock the manager asked Kleppini if he would give up, and Kleppini begged me to enter the room and release him, which I refused to do without witnesses. We then sent for the Herr Director Sidoli, Herr Reutter, and a reporter. At last Kleppini said he had the word, "Clefs," and I laughed.

"You are wrong. If you want to know the word which opens the lock, it is just what you are—'fraud.'"

And with this I grabbed his hands, quickly turned the letters till they spelled "fraud," and as they fell into their respective places he was freed.

The locks, you see, were changeable, and it required only a short moment for me to change the word. When he went into the cabinet, he tried the cuff, and it responded to the word "Clefs." While locking them on him, I changed the word to "fraud," and he, even with his eagle eye, failed to recognize that he had been trapped.

The next day, however, being a boastful man, and unwilling to acknowledge defeat, he actually circulated bills stating that he had defeated Houdini and won 5,000 marks; but the newspapers guyed him unmercifully, and published the true facts.

LIGHT ON THE SUBJECT OF JAILBREAKING AS DONE BY MY IMITATORS

I AM INDUCED TO TAKE THIS STEP FOR THE manifest reason that the public of both hemispheres may, through ignorance of the real truth, give credence to the mendacious boasts and braggadocio of the horde of imitators who have sprung into existence with mushroom rapidity of growth, and equal flimsiness of vital fiber, and who, with amazing effrontery and pernicious falsity, seek to claim and hold the credit and honor, such as they may be, that belong to me. It is in the same spirit and for the same cogent reason, that I execute my present duty of duly setting forth my right to the title which I hold and the absolute pilfering of my name, fame, and the other emoluments of success by those others who advertise and rate themselves as "Handcuff Kings," "Jail Breakers," etc., *ad libitum, ad nauseam.*

That I have a horde of imitators may not be as well known as it will be to those who have the patience and the sense of fairness sufficiently developed to lead them to read this article through to its conclusion.

Therefore, it will not be considered unbecoming of me to set forth here the details of my conception, execution, and performance of the Challenge Handcuff and Escape Act as presented by me at this time in the principal vaudeville and music hall theatres of Europe and America. And I trust also that I will not be deemed guilty of undue egoism, or of having an attack of "exaggerated ego," to borrow a popular term growing out of the Thaw trial, if I assert that this act has proved to be the greatest drawing card and longest lived sensation that has ever been offered in the annals of the stage. This has been demonstrated by the record-breaking attendance in every theatre in which I have given the act, either in part or whole, and also by the duration of my term of engagement in the principal theatres among those in which I have been booked.

"Art is long and life is short," says the ancient poet.

The stage and its people, in the light of history, make this a verity.

As examples, take the famous Davenport Brothers, also the "Georgia Magnet," also the "Bullet Proof Man," etc. For the benefit of those who have not heard of the latter sensational attraction—which was indeed a great novelty for a limited time—I will explain that the man was a German who claimed to possess a coat that was impervious to bullets. He would don this coat and allow any one to shoot a bullet of any caliber at him. Alas! One day a marksman shot him below the coat, in the groin, and he eventually died from the wounds inflicted. His last request was that his beloved invention be buried with him. This, however, was not granted, for it was thought due to the world that such an invention should be made known. The coat, on being ripped open, was found stuffed or padded with powdered glass.

Returning to the subject of my own career, I assert

here with all the positiveness I can command that I am the originator of the Challenge Handcuff Act, which consists in the artist's inviting any person into the audience to submit handcuffs of his own from which the performer must release himself. And it is proper that I should add at this point that I do not claim to have conceived and originated the simple handcuff trick. Every novice in this line knows that it has been done for many years, or so far back, as the lawyers say, "that memory runneth not to the contrary."

French historians of the stage show that as far back as early 1700, La Tude performed it. Pinetti did chain releases in 1780, and other modern magicians have had it in their programs ever since 1825. The Sr. Bologna, instructor of John Henry Anderson, made a small trick out of it. Anderson placed it among his repertoire the second time he came to America in 1861 and when exposing the Davenport Brothers, he made quite a feature of it. In fact, I have an old monthly of 1870 in which a handcuff trick is explained in an article exposing spirit mediums.

Dr. Redmond, who, I hear, is still very much alive in England, made quite a reputation as a rope expert and handcuff manipulator in 1872–3, and I have several interesting bills of his performances.

Few give me credit, but had I been able to copyright my new tricks, they would all have to pay me a royalty.

But, as such cannot be done, the only thing I ask of the numerous imitators is to give credit where credit is due.

No one, to my knowledge, performs my tests according to my method except my brother Theo Hardeen, as they ALL resort to fakery and collusion in presenting to the public that which they wish to have thought is exactly as Houdini performs his challenges.

The following challenges have been performed by myself, some of which are very interesting: Release in full view of the audience from straitjackets used on murderous insane; the nailed up in packing case escape; the packing case built on the stage; the paper bag; the willow hamper; the hamper swung in the air; the steel unprepared cage or basket; riveted into a steel water boiler; hung to a ladder in mid-air; nailed to a door; escape from unprepared glass box; out of a large football; release from a large mail pouch; escape from a roll top desk; escape from a zinc-lined piano box, etc., etc. In fact during long engagements, I have accepted a different challenge for every performance.

In order to stop all controversy concerning this jailbreaking affair, I shall publish the methods that have been used by some of those who will stop at nothing in order to willfully deceive the public.

First of all, there is a young man who calls himself Brindemour who, according to all I can learn, claims to be the originator of jail breaking and has accused me of stealing the material from him. He has even gone so far as to say that I assisted him. Why, in 1896 I visited Woonsocket, R.I. with a show and made quite a hit with the handcuff act. There I met a photographer whose name was George W. Brown. He made himself known to me and informed me that he was an amateur magician, and that at certain periods of the year he gave performances for friends and lodges. His great hit was to impersonate a ballet girl.

He showed me pictures of himself in ballet costume

and seemed to be proud that he could impersonate the female sex so perfectly. That was in 1896. About a year later, after purchasing a bunch of handcuff keys, this Brown called himself Brindemour. He gave a trial show at Keith's Providence house for Manager Lovenberg and failed to make good. His great stunt then was to make the church bells ring, which is accomplished with a confederate and was Sig. Blitz's standby. At any rate, the Great Brindemour, failing to make good, followed me into Philadelphia and started in to expose his handcuff act. He did this in Providence, also Philadelphia, and made a dismal failure. The effect of his work showed him that he was on the wrong track, and eventually he did not expose the few false tricks that he had and went into it without the exposures.

He pursued the same old groove until I returned to America, when he deliberately copied all of my challenges as best he could. I wondered how he did his jail breaking stunts, as I knew that he could no more pick a lock than the Czar of Russia will give the Russian newspapers the right of free press. Recently I have ascertained the facts as to several of his escapes, or rather their "mysterious means," and I will give the reader the benefit of my investigations. At the same time I invite the closest investigation of anything that I have ever done. While filling an engagement at Albaugh's Theatre, Baltimore, Brindemour escaped from the cells at police headquarters under the following circumstances: A reporter on the *Baltimore News*, by name of "Clint" MacCabe, called on Harry Schanberger, who is engaged in an official position at police headquarters (this incident was told me personally by Harry Schanberger and in the presence of

witnesses). MacCabe, after a chat with Harry Schahn-
berger, borrowed the set of keys from Schanberger, telling
him that he wanted to give them to Brindemour, so that
he could give a press performance and make the people
believe that Brindemour had escaped "on the square."

Schanberger loaned MacCabe the two keys, and naturally Brindemour escaped from the police headquarters'
cells, using the genuine keys that belong to the Police
Department.

AND HE DARES TO CALL HIMSELF
THE POLICE MYSTIFIER!

In mind I can almost hear the spirit of poor Chas Ber-
tram say, "Isn't that wonderful?" The strange thing about
this affair is that in Baltimore, another alleged jail breaker
met his quietus for the time being.

He is Cunning, who also labors under the delusion
that he is the original world's greatest. I quote from the
Baltimore News, Thursday February 8, 1906:

CUNNING'S GAME EXPOSED

Cunning, the hitherto mysterious opener of
handcuffs and shackles, who is exhibiting at the
Monumental Theatre this week, was found out
today by Acting Turnkey John Lanahan at the
Central Station and had to abandon the feat that
he had promised to do of escaping from a locked
cell.

Before being locked in the cell, Cunning went
into the latter, pretending to examine it, and

secretly placed a key upon a ledge, but Lanahan disovered the key just as Cunning was about to be locked in, and when told of the discovery, the wizard said, "You've got me," admitted that he could not open the cell without a key, and abandoned the exhibition.

The real truth of this jail break is that Mr. Joe Kernan went to the police captain and borrowed the keys and handed them to Cunning. The turnkey, Lanahan, not being in the "know," discovered the palpable "planting" of the keys and ran with them to the captain. In this way the "stunt" was unexpectedly exposed.

Personally, I think it ought to be a prison offense for any official to loan his keys to these would-be and so-called mystifiers, and if managers wish to lend themselves willfully to deceive their audience, the quicker they find out that they are treading the wrong path, the better for them, too. You can take any stagehand, and in five minutes make just as good a jail breaker as the many that are now trading on my name.

Another "gross" misrepresenter is a youth named Grosse. This man, or rather youth, claims that he can open time-lock safes and all the complicated locks of the world, stating that handcuffs are mere play to him. Why, he can't even pick his teeth, and if he were put to a test with a lock picker, I doubt that he could even throw back a one tumbler lock. Yes, he would have trouble to pull back a common latch.

No doubt some of the police that are entangled with some of these jail breakers will grow hot under the collar at me for showing this thing up, but as long as these fellows are pretending to do my work, and as long as they stoop to do it in this manner, just so long will I publish the real facts as soon as I find them out.

In conclusion, I wish to state that I defy any manager or police official to come forward and prove that I, by any underhanded means or conniving methods, have stooped or lowered my manhood to ask them willfully to deceive the public by such base misrepresentations.

THE COLOGNE LIBEL SUIT

Houdini reports on a trial in Cologne in 1902, in which he battled claims that he had attempted to bribe policeman Werner Graff into helping him to escape from the city's jail.

THE POLICE OF GERMANY ARE VERY STRICT IN matters of false billing or misrepresenting exhibitions to the public, and so when the Cologne police claimed that I was travelling about misrepresenting, and that my performance was "swindle", and when Schutzmann Werner Graff published a false story in the *Rheinische Zeitung*, which put me in a very bad light, as a man of honor I could not overlook the insult.

Claiming that I had been slandered, I asked for an apology and a retraction of the false stories which all the press of Germany had copied, but I was simply laughed at for my trouble.

I engaged the best lawyer of Cologne, Herr Rechtsanwalt Dr. Schreiber, Louisenstrasse 17, and commenced suit.

The first trial occurred in Cologne, February 19, 1902. I charged that Schutzmann Werner Graff had publicly slandered me, whereupon, as answer, Herr Graff told the judge and jury that he was willing to prove that

I was misrepresenting, and that he could chain me so that I could not release myself. I permitted myself to be chained by Herr Transport Police Lott, and to show how easy it was, in the presence of the judge and jury, released myself.

After a four-day trial, I won the lawsuit, and the Cologne police were fined and were to apologize to me publicly, "in the name of the Kaiser." Instead of so doing, they took it to the higher court, "Strafkammer." At this trial they had specially manufactured a lock that was made by Master Mechanic Kroch, which when once locked, could not be opened, not even with the use of the key.

The police asked that I show my ability to open this lock after it had been locked.

I accepted the challenge and walked into the room selected by the jury where I could work unhindered, and in four minutes re-entered the courtroom and handed the judges the prepared lock *unopened*.

Again I won the lawsuit, and again it was appealed, but this time to the highest court in Germany, "Oberlandesgericht", and there the learned judges again gave me the verdict from which there was no appeal.

ROPE TIES

IN THE PAST ROPE MANIPULATIONS HAVE BEEN largely confined to the cabinet demonstrations of Spirit Mediums, but the value of such material to magicians can hardly be overestimated. Witness the case of the dean of magicians, Harry Kellar, for instance, whose anti-spiritual cabinet séance was world-famous, and yet this classic was built around a single rope tie. The following pages contain practical ties that possess an entertainment value, and the majority of them may be acquired with but little practice. None of them should be attempted before an audience, however, until the details are thoroughly mastered...

Rope ties have one distinct advantage over all other forms of escape, namely, no possible suspicion is attached to the ropes themselves. In many cases where locks, chains, handcuffs, trunks, pillories and the like are used, the apparatus is more or less under suspicion, but where ordinary ropes or tapes are the only means employed, the performer gets all the credit for the escape. Where tapes can be substituted it is generally best to use them, as they create even less mistrust than ropes...

The first thing for the performer to ascertain is, if any member of the committee has followed the sea, or for any other reason is familiar with knots. If such a one is found he should be used for tests where difficult knots and secure binding does not interfere with the effect. By all means, when possible, get a physician on the committee, as it always creates a good impression to have him examine the hands, wrists, arms and shoulders, and have him report to the audience that there is no way of contracting the bones and muscles so as to slip out of the knots.

The program should be so arranged that each effect will appear a little more difficult than the preceding one, finishing with something showy and apparently difficult. The clothesline tie is particularly good for an effective finale.

Don't lose confidence in an effect because it has been presented many times before. An old trick in "good hands" is always new. Just see to it that yours are "Good hands."

Don't allow yourself to "go stale" on your act. Keep up your enthusiasm! There is nothing more contagious than exuberant enthusiasm, and it is sure to "get" an audience.

A SIMPLE RELEASE

This is perhaps the oldest release known to the Conjuring profession, the effect being to release the hands when they are tied behind the back in the ordinary way.

Although simple it is by no means easy, and will require considerable practice in order to escape in the limited time allowed by impatient audiences, but it is a very necessary part of the escape artist's education and should be thoroughly mastered.

It is accomplished by bending the body forward and working the arms down over the hips until the hands are just behind the knees. This will seem impossible at the first trial, but keep at it and you will get the knack after a while. When the hands are in position back of the knees, sit down on the floor and cross the legs, the left above the right, work the left arm down over the left knee and withdraw the left foot and then the right from the looped arms. This brings the knotted wrists in front of the body and the knots may then be untied with the teeth.

For this tie new sash cord should be used, for two reasons, first, because it is impossible to tie very tight knots with it, and second, because its smooth surface facilitates the slipping over the hips.

THE CLOTHESLINE TIE

This is a very showy tie, and is well adapted to close a rope act. About fifty or sixty feet of sash cord is used, and the statement that it is a seventy-five foot clothesline is never disputed.

The whole secret lies in the fact that it is quite impossible to tie a man while in a standing position, with such a length of rope, so that he cannot squirm out of it with comparative ease, if the tying BEGINS AT ONE END OF THE ROPE and finishes at the other.

At the beginning of this test you should hold the rope coiled in the hand, and the first move is to uncoil the rope and have it inspected by the committee.

Then explain that there seem to be a few skeptics still, and for that reason you will give the committee "plenty of rope" and let them tie you in any manner they please. During this speech you again coil the rope, at the same time explaining to the committee quietly, that in this form it will be more easily handled, passed through the knots, etc., the object of this being to force them to begin the tying at one end. Some performers have a slipknot already tied in the end of the rope, but this is not necessary, and is rather suggestive of preparation.

It is the experience of all who have used this tie, that the first few knots are carefully tied, but after a time it will be found that the rope is being used up very slowly, and they will begin winding it around the body and making very few knots. A hint to "hurry up, as the audience is getting restive," will also induce less careful knotting, and, as they are following no regular method, and several are handling the rope, they are bound to work more or less at cross purposes.

If the committee happens to be very much in earnest, and begin to make more knots than suits you, it will be well to swell the muscles, expand the chest, slightly hunch the shoulders, and hold the arm a little away from the sides. After a little practice you will find that such artifices will enable you to baulk the most knowing ones. You should always wear a coat when submitting to this tie, as that will be found to be an added help in obtaining slack.

It is an excellent idea to practice with a couple of assistants who know the game. Let them try their best to secure you and you will get a great deal of needed experience. The actual escape is always possible, but practice is necessary in order to acquire speed in execution.

A sharp knife with a hook-shaped blade should be concealed somewhere on the person, as it may be found useful in case some of the first, carefully tied knots, prove troublesome. A short piece cut from the end of the rope will never be missed.

When the last knot is made you should turn to the audience and say: "Are you all satisfied that I am securely tied?" and then immediately answer your own question by saying, "Of course, you have to be satisfied, for the committee has done all that is possible, in fact, they have 'reached the end of their rope.'"

After being placed in the cabinet you should call attention to the fact that it has taken six or eight minutes to bind you, and ask some one to hold a watch and see how long you require to escape.

THE RUSSIAN TRANSPORT TIE

This is the restraint used by Russian officials when transporting prisoners into Siberia, and it is supposed to render them helpless during the journey; but, of course, there is no reason why a prisoner should attempt a release, as he is always under the eye of an officer, and such an act would probably earn him a severe beating.

In using this tie as a stunt, however, the release may

be classed with the easy ones. The hands are tied in any manner in front, the ropes being carried up to and around the neck. For the release you have only to bring the hands up within reach and untie the wrist knots with the teeth, and with the hands free the remainder of the knots can be readily negotiated.

Do not get the idea, however, that, because easy, this escape is not effectual. Try it before an audience after you have mastered it sufficiently to acquire a measure of speed, and you will be surprised at the enthusiasm it will cause. The spectator will not stop to think that you are working at high pitch.

I can recommend this unqualifiedly to the performer who only presents one tie.

SWORD-SWALLOWING

TO ACCOMPLISH THE SWORD-SWALLOWING
feat, it is only necessary to overcome the nausea that results from the metal's touching the mucous membrane
of the pharynx, for there is an unobstructed passage,
large enough to accommodate several of the thin blades
used, from the mouth to the bottom of the stomach.
This passage is not straight, but the passing of the sword
straightens it. Some throats are more sensitive than others, but practice will soon accustom any throat to the
passage of the blade. When a sword with a sharp point
is used the performer secretly slips a rubber cap over the
point to guard against accident.

It is said that the medical fraternity first learned of the
possibility of overcoming the sensitiveness of the pharynx
by investigating the methods of the sword-swallowers.

Cliquot, who was one of the most prominent sword-
swallowers of his time, finally "reformed" and is now a
music hall agent in England. The *Strand Magazine* (1896)
has this to say of Cliquot and his art:

Cliquot, whose name suggests the swallowing of
something much more grateful and comforting
than steel swords, is a French Canadian by birth,
and has been the admitted chief in his profession

for more than 18 years. He ran away from his home in Quebec at an early age, and joined a travelling circus bound for South America. On seeing an arrant old humbug swallow a small *machete,* in Buenos Ayres, the boy took a fancy to the performance, and approached the old humbug aforesaid with the view of being taught the business. Not having any money, however, wherewith to pay the necessary premium, the overtures of the would-be apprentice were repulsed; whereupon he set about experimenting with his own aesophagus with a piece of silver wire.

To say the preliminary training for this sort of thing is painful, is to state the fact most moderately; and even when stern purpose has triumphed over the laws of anatomy, terrible danger still remains.

On one occasion having swallowed a sword, and then bent his body in different directions, as an adventurous sensation, Cliquot found that the weapon also had bent to a sharp angle; and quick as thought, realizing his own position as well as that of the sword, he whipped it out, tearing his throat in a dreadful manner. Plainly, had the upper part of the weapon become detached, the sword swallower's career must infallibly have come to an untimely end. Again, in New York, when swallowing 14 nine-inch bayonet swords at once, Cliquot had the misfortune to have a too sceptical audience, one of whom, a medical man who ought to have known better, rushed forward and impulsively dragged out the whole bunch,

inflicting such injuries upon this peculiar enter-
tainer as to endanger his life, and incapacitate him
for months.

In one of his acts Cliquot swallows a real bayonet sword, weighted with a cross bar, and two
18-lb. dumb bells. In order to vary this performance, the sword-swallower allows only a part of
the weapon to pass into his body, the remainder
being "kicked" down by the recoil of a rifle, which
is fixed to a spike in the centre of the bar, and fired
by the performer's sister.

The last act in this extraordinary performance
is the swallowing of a gold watch. As a rule, Cliquot
borrows one, but as no timepiece was forthcoming at the private exhibition where I saw him, he
proceeded to lower his own big chronometer into
his aesophagus by a slender gold chain. Many of
the most eminent physicians and surgeons in this
country immediately rushed forward with various
instruments, and the privileged few took turns in
listening for the ticking of the watch inside the
performer's body. "Poor, outraged nature is biding
her time," remarked one physician, "but mark me,
she will have a terrible revenge sooner or later!"

Eaters of glass, tacks, pebbles, and like objects, actually
swallow these seemingly impossible things, and disgorge
them after the performance is over. That the disgorging is
not always successful is evidenced by the hospital records
of many surgical operations on performers of this class,
when quantities of solid matter are found lodged in the
stomach.

Delno Fritz was not only an excellent sword-swallower, but a good showman as well. The last time I saw him he was working the "halls" in England. I hope he saved his money, for he was a clean man with a clean reputation, and, I can truly say, he was a master in his manner of indulging his appetite for the cold steel.

Deodota, an Italian Magician, was also a sword-swallower of more than average ability. He succumbed to the lure of commercialism finally, and is now in the jewelry business in the "down-town district" of New York City.

Sword-swallowing may be harmlessly imitated by the use of a fake sword with a telescopic blade, which slides into the handle. Vosin, the Paris manufacturer of magical apparatus, made swords of this type, but they were generally used in theatrical enchantment scenes, and it is very doubtful if they were ever used by professional swallowers.

It is quite probable that the swords now most generally used by the profession, which are cut from one piece of metal—handle and all—were introduced to show that they were free from any telescoping device. Swords of this type are quite thin, less than one-eighth of an inch thick, and four or five of them can be swallowed at once. Slowly withdrawing them one at a time, and throwing them on the stage in different directions, makes an effective display.

A small, but strong, electric light bulb attached to the end of a cane, is a very effective piece of apparatus for sword swallowers, as, on a darkened stage, the passage of the light down the throat and into the stomach can be plainly seen by the audience. The medical profession now makes use of this idea.

By apparently swallowing sharp razors, a dime-museum performer, whose name I do not recall, gave a variation to the sword-swallowing stunt. This was in the later days, and the act was partly fake and partly genuine. That is to say, the swallowing was fair enough, but the sharp razors, after being tested by cutting hairs, etc., were exchanged for dull duplicates, in a manner that, in better hands, might have been effective. This chap belonged to the great army of unconscious exposers, and the "switch" was quite apparent to all save the most careless observers.

His apparatus consisted of a fancy rack on which three sharp razors were displayed, and a large bandanna handkerchief, in which there were several pockets of the size to hold a razor, the three dull razors being loaded in this. After testing the edge of the sharp razors, he pretended to wipe them, one by one, with the handkerchief, and under cover of this he made the "switch" for the dull ones, which he proceeded to swallow in the orthodox fashion. His work was crude, and the crowd was inclined to poke fun at him.

I have seen one of these performers on the street, in London, swallow a borrowed umbrella, after carefully wiping the ferrule, and then return it to its owner only slightly dampened from its unusual journey. A borrowed watch was swallowed by the same performer, and while one end of the chain hung from the lips, the incredulous onlookers were invited to place their ears against his chest and listen to the ticking of the watch, which had passed as far into the aesophagus as the chain would allow.

The following anecdote from the *Carlisle*

Journal, shows that playing with sword-swallowing is about as dangerous as playing with fire.

DISTRESSING OCCURRENCE

On Monday evening last, a man named William Dempster, a juggler of inferior dexterity while exhibiting his tricks in a public house in Botchergate, kept by a person named Purdy, actually accomplished the sad reality of one of those feats, with the semblance only of which he intended to amuse his audience. Having introduced into his throat a common table knife which he was intending to swallow, he accidentally slipped his hold, and the knife passed into his stomach. An alarm was immediately given, and surgical aid procured, but the knife had passed beyond the reach of instruments, and now remains in his stomach. He has since been attended by most of the medical gentlemen of this city; and we understand that no very alarming symptoms have yet appeared, and that it is possible he may exist a considerable time, even in this awkward state. His sufferings at first were very severe, but he is now, when not in motion, comparatively easy. The knife is 9 ½ inches long, 1 inch broad in the blade, round pointed, and a handle of bone, and may generally be distinctly felt by applying the finger to the unfortunate man's belly; but occasionally, however, from change of its situation it is not perceptible. A brief notice of the analogous case of John Dimming, an American sailor, may not be unacceptable to our readers. About the year 1799 he, in imitation of some jugglers whose exhibition he had then witnessed, in an hour of intoxication, swallowed four clasp knives such as sailors commonly use; all of which passed from him in a few days without much inconvenience. Six years afterward, he swallowed *fourteen* knives of different sizes; by these, however, he was much disordered, but recovered; and again, in a paroxysm of intoxication, he actually swallowed *seventeen,* of the effects of which he died in March, 1809. On dissection, fourteen knife blades were found remaining in his stomach, and the back spring of one penetrating through the bowel, seemed the immediate cause of his death.

Several women have adopted the profession of sword-swallowing, and some have won much more than a passing fame. Notable among these is Mlle. Edith Clifford, who is, perhaps, the most generously endowed. Possessed of more than ordinary personal charms, a refined taste for dressing both herself and her stage, and an unswerving devotion to her art, she has perfected an act that has found favor even in the Royal Courts of Europe.

Mlle. Clifford was born in London in 1884 and began swallowing the blades when only 15 years of age. During the foreign tour of the Barnum & Bailey show she joined that organization in Vienna, 1901, and remained with it for five years, and now, after eighteen years of service, she stands well up among the stars. She has swallowed a 26-inch blade, but the physicians advise her not to indulge her appetite for such luxuries often, as it is quite dangerous. Blades of 18 or 20 inches give her no trouble whatever.

In the spring of 1919 I visited the Ringling Bros., and the Barnum & Bailey Show especially to witness Mlle. Clifford's act. In addition to swallowing the customary swords and sabers she introduced such novelties as a specially constructed razor, with a blade five or six times the usual length, a pair of scissors of unusual size, a saw which is 2 ½ inches wide at the broadest point, with ugly looking teeth, although somewhat rounded at the points, and several other items quite unknown to the bill of fare of ordinary mortals. A set of ten thin blades slip easily down her throat and are removed one at a time.

The sensation of her act is reached when the point of a bayonet, 23 inches long, fastened to the breech of a cannon, is placed in her mouth and the piece discharged; the recoil driving the bayonet suddenly down her throat. The gun is loaded with a 10-gauge cannon shell.

Mlle. Clifford's handsomely arranged stage occupied the place of honor in the section devoted to freaks and specialties.

Cliquot told me that Delno Fritz was his pupil, and Mlle. Clifford claims to be a pupil of Fritz.

Deserving of honorable mention also is a native of Berlin, who bills herself as Victorina. This lady is able to swallow a dozen sharp-bladed swords at once. Of Victorina, the *Boston Herald* of December 28th, 1902, said:

> By long practice she has accustomed herself to swallow swords, daggers, bayonets, walking sticks, rods, and other dangerous articles.
>
> Her throat and food passages have become so

expansive that she can swallow three long swords almost up to the hilts, and can accommodate a dozen shorter blades.

This woman is enabled to bend a blade after swallowing it. By moving her head back and forth she may even twist instruments in her throat. To bend the body after one has swallowed a sword is a dangerous feat, even for a professional swallower. There is a possibility of severing some of the ligaments of the throat or else large arteries or veins. Victorina has already had several narrow escapes.

On one occasion, while sword-swallowing before a Boston audience, a sword pierced a vein in her throat. The blade was half-way down, but instead of immediately drawing it forth, she thrust it farther. She was laid up in a hospital for three months after this performance.

In Chicago she had a still narrower escape. One day while performing at a museum on Clark Street, Victorina passed a long thin dagger down her throat. In withdrawing it, the blade snapped in two, leaving the pointed portion some distance in the passage. The woman nearly fainted when she realized what had occurred, but, by a masterful effort, controlled her feelings. Dropping the hilt of the dagger on the floor, she leaned forward, and placing her finger and thumb down her throat, just succeeded in catching the end of the blade. Had it gone down an eighth of an inch farther her death would have been certain.

STONE-EATERS

THAT THE GENESIS OF STONE-EATING DATES back hundreds of years farther than is generally supposed, is shown by a statement in Wanley's *Wonders of the Little World*, London, 1906, Vol. II, page 58, which reads as follows:

> Anno 1006, there was at Prague a certain Silesian, who, for a small reward in money, did (in the presence of many persons) swallow down white stones to the number of thirty-six; they weighed very near three pounds; the least of them was of the size of a pigeon's egg, so that I could scarce hold them all in my hand at four times: this rash adventure he divers years made for gain, and was sensible of no injury to his health thereby.

The next man of this type of whom I find record lived over six hundred years later. This was an Italian named Francois Battalia.

Doctor Bulwer, in his *Artificial Changeling,* tells a preposterous story of Battalia's being born with two pebbles in one hand and one in the other; that he refused both the breast and the pap offered him, but ate the pebbles and continued to subsist on stones for the remainder of his life. Doctor Bulwer thus describes his manner of feeding:

> His manner is to put three or four stones into a spoon, and so putting them into his mouth together, he swallows them all down, one after another; then (first spitting) he drinks a glass of beer after them. He devours about half a peck of these stones every day, and when he clinks upon his stomach, or shakes his body, you may hear the stones rattle as if they were in a sack, all of which in twenty-four hours are resolved. Once in three weeks he voids a great quantity of sand, after which he has a fresh appetite for these stones, as we have for our victuals, and by these, with a cup of beer, and a pipe of tobacco, he has his whole subsistence...

A Spanish stone-eater exhibited at the Richmond Theater, on August 2nd, 1790, and another at a later date, at the Great Room, late Globe Tavern, corner of Craven Street, Strand.

All of these phenomenal gentry claimed to subsist entirely on stones, but their modern followers hardly dare make such claims, so that the art has fallen into disrepute.

A number of years ago, in London, I watched several performances of one of these chaps who swallowed half a hatful of stones, nearly the size of hen's eggs, and then jumped up and down, to make them rattle in his stomach. I could discover no fake in the performance, and I finally gave him two and six for his secret, which was simple enough. He merely took a dose of powerful physic to clear himself of the stones, and was then ready for the next performance.

During my engagement in 1895 with Welsh Bros. Circus I became quite well acquainted with an aged Jap of the San Kitchy Akimoto troupe and from him I learned the method of swallowing quite large objects and bringing them up again at will. For practice very small potatoes are used at first, to guard against accident; and after one has mastered the art of bringing these up, the size is increased gradually till objects as large as the throat will receive can be swallowed and returned.

I recall a very amusing incident in connection with this old chap.

In one number of the programme he sat down on the ring bank and balanced a bamboo pole, at the top of which little Massay went through the regular routine of posturings. After years spent in this work, my aged friend became so used to his job that he did it automatically, and scarcely gave a thought to the boy at the top. One warm day, however, he carried his indifference a trifle too far, and dropped into a quiet nap, from which he woke only to find that the pole was falling and had already gone too far to be recovered, but the agility of the boy saved him from injury. As my knowledge of Japanese is limited to the more polite forms, I cannot repeat the remarks of the lad.

Until a comparatively recent date, incredible as it may seem, frog-swallowers were far from uncommon on the bills of the Continental theaters. The most prominent, Norton, a Frenchman, was billed as a leading feature in the high-class houses of Europe. I saw him work at the Apollo Theater, Nuremberg, where I was to follow him in; and during my engagement at the Circus Busch, Berlin, we were on the same programme, which gave me an opportunity to watch him closely.

One of his features was to drink thirty or forty large glasses of beer in slow succession. The filled glasses were displayed on shelves at the back of the stage, and had handles so that he could bring forward two or three in each hand. When he had finished these he would return for others and, while gathering another handful, would bring up the beer and eject it into a receptacle arranged between the shelves, just below the line of vision of the audience.

Norton could swallow a number of half-grown frogs and bring them up alive. I remember his anxiety on one occasion when returning to his dressing-room; it seems he had lost a frog—at least he could not account for the entire flock—and he looked very much scared, probably at the uncertainty as to whether or not he had to digest a live frog.

The Muenchen October Fest is the annual fair at that city, and a most wonderful show it is. I have been there twice; once as the big feature with Circus Carre, in 1901, and again in 1913, with the Circus Corty Althoff. The Continental Circuses are not, like those of this country, under canvas, but show in wooden buildings. At these October Fests I saw a number of frog-swallowers, and to me they were very repulsive indeed. In fact, Norton was the only one I ever saw who presented his act in a dignified manner.

Willie Hammerstein once had Norton booked to appear at the Victoria Theater, New York, but the Society for the Prevention of Cruelty to Animals would not allow him to open; so he returned to Europe without exhibiting his art in America.

In my earlier days in the smaller theaters of America, before the advent of the B. F. Keith and E. F. Albee theaters, I occasionally ran across a sailor calling himself English Jack, who could swallow live frogs and bring them up again with apparent ease.

I also witnessed the disgusting pit act of that degenerate, Bosco, who ate living snakes, and whose act gave rise to the well-known barkers' cry *He eats 'em alive!*

During an engagement in Bolton, England, I met Billington, the official hangman, who was convinced that I could not escape from the restraint he used to secure those he was about to execute.

Much to his astonishment, I succeeded in releasing myself, but he said the time consumed was more than sufficient to spring the trap and launch the doomed soul into eternity. Billington told me that he had hardened himself to the demands of his office by killing rats with his teeth.

During my engagement at the Winter Garten, Berlin, Captain Veitro, a performer that I had known for years in America, where he worked in side shows and museums, came to Berlin and made quite a stir by eating poisons. He appeared only a few times, however, as his act did not appeal to the public, presumably for the reason that he had his stomach pumped out at each performance, to prove that it really contained the poison. This may have been instructive, but it possessed little appeal as entertainment, and I rarely heard of the venturesome captain after that.

Years ago I saw a colored poison-eater at "Worth's

Museum, New York City, who told me that he escaped the noxious effects of the drugs by eating quantities of oatmeal mush.

Another colored performer took an ordinary bottle, and, after breaking it, would bite off chunks, crunch them with his teeth, and finally swallow them. I have every reason to believe that his performance was genuine.

The beer-drinking of Norton was a more refined version of the so-called water-spouting of previous generations, in which the returning was done openly, a performance that could not fail to disgust a modern audience. To be sure, in the days of the Dime Museum, a Negro who returned the water worked those houses; but his performance met with little approval, and it is years since I have heard of such an exhibition.

The first water-spouter of whom I find a record was Blaise Manfrede or de Manfre, who toured Europe about the middle of the seventeenth century.

A pupil of Manfrede's, by the name of Floram Marchand, who seems to have been fully the equal of his master, appeared in England in 1650. The following description of Marchand's performance is from *The Book of Wonderful Characters,* edition of 1869, page 126:

In the summer of 1650, a Frenchman named Floram Marchand was brought over from Tours to London, who professed to be able to "turn water into wine," and at his vomit render not only the tincture, but the strength and smell of several wines, and several waters. He learnt the rudiments of this art from Bloise, an Italian, who not long before was questioned by Cardinal Mazarin, who threatened him with all the miseries that a tedious imprisonment could bring upon him, unless he would discover to him by what art he did it. Bloise, startled at the sentence, and fearing the event, made a full confession on these terms, that the Cardinal would communicate it to no one else.

From this Bloise, Marchand received all his instruction; and finding his teacher the more sought after in France, he came by the advice of two English friends to England, where the trick was new. Here—the cause of it being utterly unknown—he seems for a time to have gulled and astonished the public to no small extent, and to his great profit.

Before long, however, the whole mystery was cleared up by his two friends, who had probably not received the share of the profits to which they thought themselves entitled. Their somewhat circumstantial account runs as follows.

To prepare his body for so hardy a task, before he makes his appearance on the stage, he takes a pill about the quantity of a hazel nut, confected with the gall of an heifer, and wheat flour baked. After which he drinks privately in his chamber four or five pints of luke-warm water, to take all the foulness and slime from his stomach, and to avoid that loathsome spectacle which otherwise would make thick the water, and offend the eye of the observer.

In the first place, he presents you with a pail of luke-warm water, and sixteen glasses in a basket, but you are to understand that every morning he boils two ounces of Brazil thin-sliced in three pints of running water, so long till the whole strength and color of the Brazil is exhausted: of this he drinks half a pint in his private chamber before he comes on the stage: you are also to understand that he neither eats nor drinks in the morning on those days when he comes on the stage, the cleansing pill and water only excepted; but in the evening will make a very good supper, and eat as much as two or three other men who have not their stomachs so thoroughly purged.

Before he presents himself to the spectators, he washes all his glasses in the best white-wine vinegar he can procure. Coming on the stage, he always washes his first glass, and rinses it two or three times, to take away the strength of the vinegar, that it may in no wise discolour the complexion of what is represented to be wine.

At his first entrance, he drinks four and twenty glasses of luke-warm water, the first vomit he makes the water seems to be a full deep claret: you are to observe that his gall-pill in the morning, and so many glasses of luke-warm water afterwards, will force him into a sudden capacity to vomit, which vomit upon so much warm water, is for the most part so violent on him, that he cannot forbear if he would.

You are again to understand that all that comes from him is red of itself, or has a tincture of it from the first Brazil water; but by degrees, the more water he drinks, as on every new trial he drinks as many glasses of water as his stomach will contain, the water that comes from him will grow paler and paler. Having then made his essay on claret, and proved it to be of the same complexion, he again drinks four or five glasses of luke-warm water, and brings forth claret and beer at once into two several glasses: now you are to observe that the glass which appears to be claret is rinsed as before, but the beer glass not rinsed at all, but is still moist with the white-wine vinegar, and the first strength of the Brazil water being lost, it makes the water which he vomits up to be of a more pale colour, and much like our English beer.

He then brings his rouse again, and drinks up fifteen or sixteen glasses of luke-warm water, which the pail will plentifully afford him: he will not bring you up the pale Burgundian wine, which, though more faint of complexion than the claret, he will tell you is the purest wine in Christendom. The strength of the Brazil water, which he took immediately before his appearance on the stage, grows fainter and fainter. This glass, like the first glass in which he brings forth his claret, is washed, the better to represent the colour of the wine therein.

The next he drinks comes forth sack from him, or according to that complexion. Here he does not wash his glass at all; for the strength of the vinegar must alter what is left of the complexion of the Brazil water, which he took in the morning before he appeared on the stage.

You are always to remember, that in the interim, he will commonly drink up four or five glasses of the luke-warm water, the better to provoke his stomach to a disgorgement, if the first rouse will not serve turn. He will now (for on every disgorge he will bring you forth a new colour), he will now present you with white wine. Here also he will not wash his glass, which (according to the vinegar in which it was washed) will give it a colour like it. You are to understand, that when he gives you the colour of so many wines, he never washes the glass, but at his first evacuation, the strength of the vinegar being no wise compatible with the colour of the Brazil water.

Having performed this task, he will then give you a show of rose-water; and this indeed, he does so cunningly, that it is not the show of rose-water, but rosewater itself. If you observe him, you will find that either behind the pail where his luke-warm water is, or behind the basket in which his glasses are, he will have on purpose a glass of rose-water prepared for him. After he has taken it, he will make the spectators believe that he drank nothing but the luke-warm water out of the pail; but he saves the rose-water in the glass, and holding his hand in an indirect way, the people believe, observing the water dropping from his fingers, that it is nothing but the water out of the pail. After this he will drink four or five glasses more out of the pail, and then comes up the rose-water, to the admiration of the beholders. You are to understand, that the heat of his body working with his rose-water gives a full and fragrant smell to all the water that comes from him as if it were the same.

The spectators, confused at the novelty of the

sight, and looking and smelling on the water, immediately he takes the opportunity to convey into his hand another glass; and this is a glass of Angelica water, which stood prepared for him behind the pail or basket, which having drunk off, and it being furthered with four or five glasses of luke-warm water, out comes the evacuation, and brings with it a perfect smell of the Angelica, as it was in the rose-water above specified.

To conclude all, and to show you what a man of might he is, he has an instrument made of tin, which he puts between his lips and teeth; this instrument has three several pipes, out of which, his arms a-kimbo, a putting forth himself, he will throw forth water from him in three pipes, the distance of four or five yards. This is all clear water, which he does with so much port and such a flowing grace, as if it were his master-piece.

He has been invited by divers gentlemen and personages of honour to make the like evacuation in milk, as he made a semblance in wine. You are to understand that when he goes into another room, and drinks two or three pints of milk. On his return, which is always speedy, he goes first to his pail, and afterwards to his vomit. The milk which comes from him looks curdled, and shows like curdled milk and drink. If there be no milk ready to be had, he will excuse himself to his spectators, and make a large promise of what he will perform the next day, at which time being sure to have milk enough to serve his turn, he will perform his promise.

His milk he always drinks in a withdrawing room, that it may not be discovered, for that
would be too apparent, nor has he any other shift
to evade the discerning eye of the observers.

It is also to be considered that he never comes
on the stage (as he does sometimes three or four
times in a day) but he first drinks the Brazil water,
without which he can do nothing at all, for all that
comes from him has a tincture of the red, and it
only varies and alters according to the abundance
of water which he takes, and the strength of the
white-wine vinegar, in which all the glasses are
washed.

DEFIERS OF POISONOUS REPTILES

ABOUT TWENTY-TWO YEARS AGO, DURING ONE
of my many engagements at Kohl and Middleton's, Chicago, there appeared at the same house a marvelous
"rattle-snake poison defier" named Thardo. I watched
her act with deep interest for a number of weeks, never
missing a single performance. For the simple reason that
I worked within twelve feet from her, my statement that
there was absolutely no fake attached to her startling performance can be taken in all seriousness, as the details
are still fresh in my mind.

Thardo was a woman of exceptional beauty, both of
form and feature, a fluent speaker and a fearless enthu-
siast in her devotion to her art. She would allow herself
to be repeatedly bitten by rattle-snakes and received no
harm excepting the ordinary pain of the wound. After
years of investigation I have come to the belief that this
immunity was the result of an absolutely empty stomach, into which a large quantity of milk was taken shortly
after the wound was inflicted, the theory being that the
virus acts directly on the contents of the stomach, chang-
ing it to a deadly poison.

It was Thardo's custom to give weekly demonstrations of this power, to which the medical profession

were invited, and on these occasions she was invariably greeted with a packed house. When the moment of the supreme test came, an awed silence obtained; for the thrill of seeing the serpent flash up and strike possessed a positive fascination for her audiences. Her bare arms and shoulders presented a tempting target for the death-dealing reptile whose anger she had aroused. As soon as he had buried his fangs in her expectant flesh, she would coolly tear him from the wound and allow one of the physicians present to extract a portion of the venom and immediately inject it into a rabbit, with the result that the poor creature would almost instantly go into convulsions and would soon die in great agony.

Another rattlesnake defier is a resident of San Antonio, Texas. Her name is Learn, and she once told me that she was the preceptor of Thardo. This lady deals in live rattle-snakes and their by-products—rattle-snake skin, which is used for fancy bags and purses; rattle-snake oil, which is highly esteemed in some quarters as a specific for rheumatism; and the venom, which has a pharmaceutical value.

She employs a number of men as snake trappers. Their usual technique is to pin the rattler to the ground by means of a forked stick thrust dexterously over his neck, after which he is conveyed into a bag made for the purpose. Probably the cleverest of her trappers is a Mexican who has a faculty of catching these dangerous creatures with his bare hands. The story goes that this chap has been bitten so many times that the virus no longer has any effect on him. Even that most poisonous of all reptiles, the Gila monster, has no terrors for him. He swims along the shore where venomous reptiles most abound, and fearlessly attacks any and all that promise any income to his employer.

In a very rare book by General Sir Arthur Thurlow Cunynghame, entitled, *My Command in South Africa,* 1880, I find the following:

> The subject of snake bites is one of no small interest in this country.
>
> Liquid ammonia is, *par excellence,* the best antidote. It must be administered immediately after the bite, both internally, diluted with water, and externally, in its concentrated form.
>
> The "Eau de luce" and other nostrums sold for this purpose have ammonia for their main ingredient. But it generally happens in the case of a snake bite that the remedy is not at hand, and hours may elapse before it can be obtained. In this case the following treatment will work well. Tie a ligature tightly *above* the bite, scarify the wound deeply with a knife, and press either pleasure or pain at his will. Some were purchased by individuals, and Jack pocketed his gains, observing, "A frog, or a mouse, occasionally, is enough for a snake's satisfaction."
>
> The *Naturalist's Cabinet* says that "In presence of the Grand Duke of Tuscany, while the philosophers were making elaborate dissertations on the danger of the poison of vipers, taken inwardly, a viper catcher, who happened to be present, requested that a quantity of it might be put into a vessel; and then, with the utmost confidence, and to the astonishment of the whole company, he

drank it off. Everyone expected the man instantly to drop down dead; but they soon perceived their mistake, and found that, taken inwardly, the poison was as harmless as water."

William Oliver, a viper catcher at Bath, was the first who discovered that, by the application of olive oil, the bite of the viper is effectually cured. On the first of June, 1735, he suffered himself to be bitten by an old black viper; and after enduring the agonizing symptoms of approaching death, by using olive oil he perfectly recovered.

Vipers' flesh was formerly esteemed for its medicinal virtues, and its salt was thought to exceed every other animal product in giving vigor to a languid constitution.

According to Cornelius Heinrich Agrippa (called Agrippa of Nettesheim), a German philosopher, and student of alchemy and magic, who was born in 1486, and died in 1535, "If you would handle adders and snakes without harm, wash your hands in the juice of radishes, and you may do so without harm."

Even though it may seem a digression, I yield to the temptation to include here an extraordinary "snake story" taken from *An Actor Abroad,* which Edmund Leathes published in 1880:

I will here relate the story of a sad death—I might feel inclined to call it suicide—which occurred in Melbourne shortly before my arrival in the colonies. About a year previous to the time of which I am now writing, a gentleman of birth and education, a Cambridge B.A., a barrister by profession and a literary man by choice, with his wife and three children emigrated to Victoria. He arrived in Melbourne with one hundred and fifty pounds in his pocket, and hope unlimited in his heart.

Poor man! He, like many another man, quickly discovered that muscles in Australia are more marketable than brains. His little store of money began to melt under the necessities of his wife and family. To make matters worse he was visited by a severe illness. He was confined to his bed for some weeks, and during his convalescence his wife presented him with another of those "blessings to the poor man," a son.

It was Christmas time, his health was thoroughly restored, he naturally possessed a vigorous constitution; but his heart was beginning to fail him, and his funds were sinking lower and lower.

At last one day, returning from a long and solitary walk, he sat down with pen and paper and made a calculation by which he found he had sufficient money left to pay the insurance upon his life for one year, which, in the case of his death occurring within that time, would bring to his widow the sum of three thousand pounds. He went to the insurance office, and made his application—was examined by the doctor—the policy was made out, his life was insured. From that day he grew moody and morose, despair had conquered hope.

At this time a snake-charmer came to Melbourne, who advertised a wonderful cure for snake-bites. This charmer took one of the halls in the town, and there displayed his livestock, which consisted of a great number of the most deadly and venomous snakes which were to be found in India and Australia.

This man had certainly some most wonderful antidote to the poison of a snake's fangs. In his exhibitions he would allow a cobra to bite a dog or a rabbit, and, in a short time after he had applied his nostrum the animal would thoroughly revive; he advertised his desire to perform upon humanity, but, of course, he could find no one fool enough to risk his life so unnecessarily.

The advertisement caught the eye of the unfortunate emigrant, who at once proceeded to the hall where the snake charmer was holding his exhibition. He offered himself to be experimented upon; the fanatic snake-charmer was delighted, and an appointment was made for the same evening as soon as the "show" should be over.

The evening came; the unfortunate man kept his appointment, and, in the presence of several witnesses, who tried to dissuade him from the trial, bared his arm and placed it in the cage of an enraged cobra and was quickly bitten. The nostrum was applied apparently in the same manner as it had been to the lower animals which had that evening been experimented upon, but whether it was that the poor fellow willfully did something to prevent its taking effect—or whatever the reason—he soon became insensible, and in a couple of hours he was taken home to his wife and family—a corpse. The next morning the snake-charmer had flown, and left his snakes behind him.

The insurance company at first refused payment of the policy, asserting that the death was suicide; the case was tried and the company lost it, and the widow received the three thousand pounds. The snake-charmer was sought in vain; he had the good fortune and good sense to be seen no more in the Australian colonies.

As several methods of combating the effects of poisons have been mentioned in the foregoing pages, I feel in duty bound to carry the subject a little farther and present a list of antidotes. I shall not attempt to educate my readers in the art of medicine, but simply to give a list of such ordinary materials as are to be found in practically every household, materials cited as antidotes for the more common poisons. I have taken them from the best authorities obtainable and they are offered in the way of first aid, to keep the patient alive till the doctor arrives; and if they should do no good, they can hardly do harm.

The first great rule to be adopted is *send for the doctor at once* and give him all possible information about the case without delay. Use every possible means to keep the patient at a normal temperature. When artificial respiration is necessary, always get hold of the tongue and pull it well forward in order to keep the throat clear, then turn the patient over on his face and press the abdomen to force out the air, then turn him over on the back so that the lungs may fill again, repeating this again and again till the doctor arrives. The best stimulants are strong tea or coffee; but when these are not sufficient, a tablespoon of brandy, whisky, or wine may be added.

Vegetable and mineral poisons, with few exceptions, act as efficiently in the blood as in the stomach. Animal poisons act only through the blood, and are inert when introduced into the stomach. Therefore there is absolutely no danger in sucking the virus from a snake bite, except that the virus should not be allowed to touch any spot where the skin is broken.

CRYPTOGRAPHY

MY FIRST INTRODUCTION TO THE WORLD OF cryptography occurred about twenty years ago when, not having enough money to wire home for my return fare, I was stranded with a small touring company in Chetopa, Kansas. I wished to leave that beautiful city as fast as the inventions of mankind would permit me. But alas! I lacked sufficient money with which to buy a postage stamp, let alone railroad fare, so I went to the telegraph office to send a message "collect at the other end." After a long conversation with one of the clerks or operators, he accepted my wire, and I sat down to wait for an answer from "Home, Sweet, Home."

While I was waiting, an old man walked into the office and handed in a message, paid for it, and left the office. No sooner was he gone than the operator called me to him and said, "Here, you magician, tell me what this means.

I shall never forget the message; it was of such a nature that it is almost impossible to forget it. The operator looked at me with a smile and said that he would send the message and then allow me to study it while I waited for my answer.

I was in that office at least five hours, and to that wait

I am indebted for my ability today to read almost any cipher or secret writing that is handed to me. I have made quite a study of this art, and often it has been the means of giving me a friendly warning or clever hint to look out for myself.

The message that I studied in that grim telegraph station was written as follows:

"XNTQLZCXHM FOKDZRDQDS
TQMZRJGDQ SNEN QFHUDE ZSGDQ."

I managed, after some worry, to solve the message, and very few things in after life gave me as much pleasure as did the unraveling of that code. I noticed that by putting one letter for another, I eventually spelled the entire message, which read as follows: "Your ma dying; please return; ask her to forgive. Father."

The telegraph operator seemed to think that this was a great feat, and even while we talked about it the answer arrived:

"BZTFGSDWOQ DRRZQQHUDMNN
MXNTQKHSSKD ZKHBD."

Which reads: "Caught express; arrive noon. Your little Alice." This is a very simple cipher, and all there is to it is to alter the alphabet, and instead of writing the letter required, simply write the letter in front of it. For instance, if writing the word "yes" according to your code, you will have to write "XDR." Note: It is necessary to use "Z" for the letter "A."

This was my debut as a cypher-ist. Since then I have picked up the newspapers and have never failed to read any and all cyphers printed in the personal columns. Sometimes, I have in a joking manner answered their cypher and signed myself "Roger Bacon," as he was the first I know of to make use of this method of varying the alphabet.

A brief narrative of cryptography may not be out of place. The word cryptography is derived from the Greek. There seem to be two words used, *kryptos* and *graphein*, the first meaning "something that is concealed or hidden;" the second meaning, in plain English, "to write." Both together naturally mean to be able to communicate with others in a secret manner which to the uninitiated means nothing, but to the initiated, has all kinds of meaning.

Our second sight artists were the first to utilize the code or cipher for exhibitions. They had secret signs, movements, and questions in which they conveyed their answers or information to the medium. Horse, dog, and animal trainers train their troupes with signs that to the public are almost imperceptible. I know of several cases where the animal is so well trained that no man has ever been able to catch the trainer in their movements. Mazeppa, an American horse, while in England, was supposed to be a wonderful mathematician, and it was published that the horse was once known to have studied arithmetic. Maguire, the trainer, was formerly an expert accountant and had several peculiar signs for his horse that he could give either behind the animal or at the side. From what I can learn, a horse has wonderful eyesight; he can see in back of himself quite a distance.

I don't mean looking backward, but from the position of his eyes, he manages to see quite a good deal of what is going on behind him.

Der Kluge Hans, a horse trained in Germany by some very well-known gentlemen, fooled the learned professors a long time, and it was only through a certain Baumeister, who was a friend of Herr Dir— of the Circus in Berlin, that the horse was exposed. This man had the horse trained in such an ace manner that his method was never discovered. He must have had his groom in the secret, for the horse would answer all questions correctly, but I think the groom gave Der Kluge Hans the signals. It created the biggest sensation that has ever taken place in Germany in the animal world.

This is how the trick was exposed: Baumeister came to the exhibition and wanted the horse to tell him the time. Now as it was claimed that the horse could tell it himself, the owner would look to see if the horse was correct. But this time, the owner was not allowed to look at the watch, nor was any one else, and Der Kluge Hans stood there Der Dumme Hans. This led to an argument, and Baumeister was asked in a manner more forcible than elegant, to vacate the building, which he did. The incident proved the Waterloo of the horse as well as the owner.

Dogs are trained to obey at the snapping of the fingernails one against the other, and I have an old bill where a goose and pig play a game of cards together, and the goose always beats the pig.

SCYTALA LACONIAS

But I wander from my subject. Roger Bacon thought so much of cryptography that he classed it under the name of cyphers as a part of grammar. The Lacedemonians, according to Plutarch, had a method in which a round stick is made use of. John Baptiste Porta (1658) also described this method, so I will show the reader just what there is in it. This method is sometimes attributed to Archimedes but as to that, I am in no position to argue one way or the other. For this system, you must obtain two round sticks, one being in your possession and the other in the possession of the person to whom you wish to send your message. A long and narrow strip of paper, say ticker tape, must be wrapped or rolled spirally across your stick or cylinder. Now write your message right across the strips. When unrolled, the slips of paper seem to signify nothing. These wooden sticks are known as Scytala Laconias.

CHECKER BOARD CIPHER

The method of using numbered squares is sometimes called the checker-board system, and with this method, you can arrange almost any code in the world, using any article, places, or characters, as you simply use the checker board as your guide, and arrange everything accordingly.

It is possible to hold a conversation by knocks on the

walls of cells, but in America, where they seldom have solid walls in prisons or station houses, it is sometimes used by holding up figures and spelling out the words, although the deaf and dumb alphabet is far better, but harder to learn. I mean by that, it can't be learned in the first lesson, while with a chart, this checker board is a very easy matter. Criminals have their own hieroglyph-ics, in fact you will find secret signs and marks in almost every path of life.

Although you can find a great many ways and means of deciphering secret codes, the most reliable rules and those that will enable you to read any of the common cyphers used in the English language, are as follows: First find out which letter, number, or character is used most frequently, which you can set down as being one of the vowels. The letter "e" is used more than any other letter. The vowel used the least is the letter "u." You can also place "y" with your vowels as that letter will be certain of being used many times and often will denote the end of a word.

In the words of three letters, there are most com-monly two consonants, such as: the, and, not, but, yet, for, why, all, you, she, his, her, our, who, may, can, did, was, are, has, had, let, one, two, six, ten, etc.

The most common words of four letters are: this, that, then, with, when, from, here, some, most, none, they, them, whom, mine, your, must, will, have, been, were, four, five, nine, etc.

The most usual words of five letters are: there, these, those, which, while, since, their, shall, might, could, would, ought, three, seven, eight, etc.

Words of two or more syllables frequently begin with

two consonants or with a prefix, that is, a vowel joined with one or two consonants. The most common double consonants are: bl, br, dr, fl, fr, gl, ph, pl, sh, sp, st, th, tr, wh, wr, etc., and the most common prefixes are: com, con, de, dif, ex, im, in, int, mis, par, pre, pro, re, sub, sup, un, etc. The two consonants most frequently used at the ends of long words are: ck, ld, lf, mn, nd, ng, rl, rm, rn, rp, rt, sm, st, xt, etc., while the commonest terminations are: ed, en, et, es, er, ing, ly, son, sion, tion, able, ence, ent, ment, full, less, ness, etc.

The vowels that are used most frequently together are "ea" and "ou." The most common consonant at the ends of words is "s," and next in use will be "r" and "t."

Any time two similar characters come together, they are most likely to be the two consonants "f," "l," or "s," or the vowels "e" or "o." The letter that precedes or follows two similar characters is either a vowel or "l," "m," "n," or "r." In deciphering, begin with the words that consist of a single letter, which will be either "a," "i," or "o." Then take the words of two letters, one of which will be a vowel. Of these words, the most frequent are: an, to, be, by, of, on, or, no, so, as, at, if, in, it, he, me, my, us, we, and am.

In making use of a cypher, it must be understood that the longer the message is, the easier it is to decipher. And the message should be written without any space with all the letters close together. This will make it much more difficult to decipher.

To give you an idea of how important the letter "e" is in all writings, the following inscription over the Decalogue in a country church runs as follows:

PRSRVYPRFCTMNVRKPTHSPRCPTSTN.

It is stated that this was not read in over two hundred years, but if you will insert the letter "e" in a good many spaces, you will be able to read, "Preserve, ye perfect men; ever keep these precepts ten."

Merchants use words of ten letters for their trade or secret marks, but they are very simple to read. All you have to do is to get the worth of their prices for a few of their articles, and before you have six figures, you can read the rest as easily as the merchant or clerks themselves. Some of the words that I have known to be in actual use are French lady, with lucky, fishmarket, etc.

It is as well to say here that the methods shown in my articles are not by any means a complete compilation. I have only collected some of the best methods and trust that it will repay the reader to study one or the other, as you can never tell when it may come in handy to give your friend or assistant some secret sign or gesture which your enemy will not understand. Some future day, I shall publish all the silent codes that I have met and those that are being made use of by second sight artists, but for the present moment, I trust this effort will suffice.

THE RIGHT WAY TO DO WRONG

O would the deed were good!
For now the Devil, that told me I did well,
Says that this deed is chronicled in Hell!
                              —*Shakespeare*

THERE IS AN UNDER WORLD—A WORLD OF
cheat and crime—a world whose highest good is successful evasion of the laws of the land.

You who live your life in placid respectability know but little of the real life of the denizens of this world. The daily records of the police courts, the startling disclosures of fraud and swindle in newspaper stories are about all the public know of this world of crime. Of the real thoughts and feelings of the criminal, of the terrible fascination which binds him to his nefarious career, of the thousands—yea, tens of thousands—of undiscovered crimes and unpunished criminals, you know but little.

The object of this book is twofold: First, to safeguard the public against the practices of the criminal classes by exposing their various tricks and explaining the adroit methods by which they seek to defraud. "Knowledge is power" is an old saying. I might paraphrase it in this case by saying knowledge is safety. I wish to put the public on its guard, so that honest folks may be able to detect and protect themselves from the dishonest, who labor under the false impression that it is easier to live dishonestly than to thrive by honest means.

In the second place, I trust this book will afford entertaining, as well as instructive reading, and that the facts and experiences, the exposés and explanations here set forth may serve to interest you, as well as put you in a position where you will be less liable to fall a victim.

The material contained in this book has been collected by me personally during many years of my active professional life. It has been my good fortune to meet personally and converse with the chiefs of police and the most famous detectives in all the great cities of the world. To these gentlemen I am indebted for many amusing and instructive incidents hitherto unknown to the world.

The work of collecting and arranging this material and writing the different chapters has occupied many a leisure hour. My only wish is that *The Right Way to Do Wrong* may amuse and entertain my readers and place the unwary on their guard. If my humble efforts in collecting and writing these facts shall accomplish this purpose, I shall be amply repaid, and feel that my labor has not been in vain.

HARRY HOUDINI,
Handcuff King and Jail Breaker.

INCOME OF A CRIMINAL

People of respectability and inexperience, who have no knowledge of the criminal classes, usually imagine that every criminal is a hardened villain, incapable of even the ordinary feelings of family affection, and that of necessity the professional crook, thief, or burglar is uneducated and ignorant.

In fact, nothing could be more remote from the truth. Do you see that well-dressed, respectable-looking man glancing over the editorial page of the *Sun*? You would be surprised to know that he is a professional burglar and that he has a loving wife and a family of children who little know the "business" which takes him away for many days and nights at a time.

You meet a grave and benevolent-looking gentleman on a railway train; perhaps he shares your seat and interests you by his brilliant and intelligent conversation. You little suspect that he is at the head of a gang of the most expert bank burglars in the country.

As a matter of fact, some of the brightest brains and keenest minds belong to professional criminals. They live by their wits and must needs keep those wits sharp and active. Not that I would have you think that all professional criminals go about in the guise of gentlemen. There are all grades of culture and lack of culture in the various nefarious callings of crime. The sneak thief and the burglar may and often does look the "hard citizen" he is; but you will never find him lacking in a certain kind of quick wits and a certain kind of brain power. So highly organized is the machinery of the law and police protection in our modern civilization that one of the first requisites for success as a professional criminal is brains.

DOES IT PAY TO COMMIT CRIME?

This is a question I have often asked the chiefs of police and great detectives of every country in the world. How great are the money rewards of evil doing? Does a "good" burglar have an income equal to that of a bank president? Can a pickpocket make more money than the fashionable tailor who makes the pockets? Is a gambler better paid than a governor? Can a shoplifter make more money than the saleswoman? In fact, does it pay to be a criminal, and, if so, how great is the reward for evil doing?

I am aware that it is the general impression, considered simply as a matter of profits, that the professional criminal is well paid. He gets something for nothing; therefore you would say at a first glance that he must be rolling in wealth.

Many people who get their ideas of criminals from novels and story papers, for instance, imagine a gambler as a man who always has a roll of bills in his pocket big enough to choke a horse, as they say. No doubt, also, the histories of sensational coups as reported in the daily press are chiefly responsible for this false impression. But such colossal frauds and robberies are rarely the work of professional criminals. They are usually perpetrated by men whose previous good character has placed them in positions of trust. Men who have led honest lives, when temptation came along and on paper they figured out that they could not lose—why, they stole and fell—into the clutches of the law. Disgraced, they are ruined for life, often ruining all their family. It is a terrible thing to have the finger of fate point at you with the remark, "His father is serving time for doing so and so," or "Her brother is now in his sixteenth year, and comes out in five years."

Such humble criminals as the area sneak thief, the porch and hallway thieves, and the ordinary shoplifter may be dismissed with a few words; their gains are miserably small, they live in abject poverty, and after detection (for sooner or later they are detected) they end their lives in the workhouse.

"If I could earn $5 a week honest, I'd gladly give up 'dragging' [shoplifting]," said a thief of this type to a New York detective; "but I can't stand regular work, never could; it's so much easier to 'prig' things." No avarice, but simple laziness keeps these thieves dishonest.

More lucrative are the callings of the counter thief, the pickpocket, and the "buzzer" or watch thief. Of those the pickpocket wins the largest returns. A purse hunter who knows his work would think he had wasted his time if he did not make $5 on an evening stroll. Race meetings and fairs may bring him in $100 to $150 a day, but: an average day's makings amount to only $8 to $12.

The passing of bad money, as everyone knows who is behind the scenes in criminal life, is a very poorly paid "industry," while the punishment risked is heavy. In England the "snide pitchers" or "shovers of the queer," as they were called, used to buy the counterfeit coins at so much a dozen, and, working in pairs, pass them out in shops.

Highwaymen, robbers, and hold-up men sometimes make big hauls, but their careers are short. Into their brutal hands pass many a diamond pin or ring, many a gold chain, worth $20 or $25, even at melting-pot prices of some dishonest goldsmith. Happily for society, these ruffians are speedily brought to book and their ill-gotten gains are dearly earned. There is a thieves' proverb which runs, "A six months' run and the hook (thief) is done." The garrote and hold-up men have far shorter lease of liberty and frequently fall into the clutches of the law within a day or two after release from prison.

Both burglars and confidence men may make big coups occasionally, but their income is precarious. The burglar is at the mercy of the "fence," as the receiver of stolen goods is called, and realizes only a small part of the actual value of his pelf. I suppose a burglar would be considered very successful if he made $3,000 a year actual profit. The "fence" has much larger opportunities and his voracity is well known. A detective friend was well acquainted with one who made as much as $5,000 a year for several years and finally shot himself to avoid arrest. Another "fence" actually amassed a fortune, but his wealth did not prevent him from dying miserably in prison.

The truth is, that a life of dishonesty may pay at first when you are not known to the police, but when an offender once falls into the hands of the ever-watchful police he begins to be a well-known customer. He now pays dearer and dearer every time he is brought up for trial. His brief spells of liberty are spent in committing some crime that once again brings him back to the prison, so when you figure out the sentences he has to serve, why, his honest gains are contemptible compared to such awful penalties. . .

In order to put a finish to this chapter, it can be said that IT DOES NOT PAY TO LEAD A DISHON-EST LIFE, and to those who read this book, although it will inform them "The Right Way to Do Wrong," all I have to say is one word and that is "DON'T."

PROFESSIONAL BURGLARY

The professional burglar is a man of resources and daring. He has usually had a long training in criminal pursuits. A good burglar is a man who knows how to keep his own counsel and is very careful how he tells his plans to any one else.

If the same amount of ability and talent that many a criminal exercises to become a professional burglar were applied to an honest pursuit, he would gain wealth and fame; but once started in the path of crime it is difficult to turn aside.

The burglar who makes the breaking into houses a profession is held by the fascination of the danger and the rewards of his pursuit. The consciousness that he is able to accomplish the almost impossible, to plan and bring off coups which fill the newspapers with flare headings, is as much a matter of pride to him as high attainments in an honorable profession are to another man.

Planning a Bold Break. When a burglar starts out on a job he does not do it haphazardly. He carefully selects a house in a favorable location, occupied by a family who are known to have valuable possessions worth taking away. The retired location of the house, the ease of access, every approach and every avenue of escape if detected are carefully studied. Then he goes about acquainting himself with the habits of the people who occupy the house. He soon knows when they come and go, how the doors are fastened, how the windows are secured. Perhaps he ingratiates himself by paying marked attention to the maids of the kitchen, and so earns the inside workings of the household. Usually this is accomplished by the aid of a confederate or member of the gang to which he belongs, and if he can induce the cooperation of some servant his work is made so much the easier.

At length the night of the burglary arrives. The date has been carefully set. You may be sure that there is not a full moon to illuminate the grounds, as he has consulted the almanac. If there is a watchdog, the burglar carries ample means to quiet him, in the shape of a small bottle of chloroform. Accompanied by his pal (for most of these burglars work in pairs) they rapidly effect their entrance in accordance with their plan. Usually one man is stationed outside, to give warning by means of a peculiar whistle or other sound in case detection is to be feared.

How the burglar overcomes all the obstacles of his entrance into the house will be treated later, but to a professional cracksman the ordinary locks of doors, the ordinary window fastenings and safety arrangements that the householder attends to so carefully every night offer but little or no obstacle. When the time comes for him to enter, he enters as quietly and quickly as though he were the master himself—in fact, very much more quietly. Once inside, his glimmering electric dark lantern, which can be hooded in an instant, gives him sufficient light to move with noiseless rubber-soled shoes to the different apartments. The absolute silence in which a professional cracksman can go through a house, avoiding creaking doors, and escaping every loose board which may betray his presence is astonishing. Many a householder has awakened in the morning find his house rifled who would deem it impossible for anyone to enter his house, much less his room, without immediately arousing him.

To show how carefully a burglar plans for the "cracking" of some specially desirable "crib," one ex-convict declares that he has often expended large sums of money in making the preliminary arrangements for some great coup. If a burglar should happen to be caught in the house-breaking act, it is fairly important that he should not be recognized afterwards; so most professional burglars are very careful to provide themselves with a disguise when out on their "work." One reformed criminal told Inspector Byrnes that he had several times been seen by people while entering houses, but they had never once been able to recognize him afterwards. His simple plan he described as follows: "I always wore a specially made wig, with false side-whiskers and moustache of the best quality. My wardrobe was extensive, and contained reversible coats and reversible trousers, after the style used by quick-change artists on the stage. With the aid of these, I have been able to make a complete change of appearance in less than two minutes." It is easy to see how rogues take more pains to perpetrate robberies than honest men do to get a living.

The Burglar Who Walked Backward. A London burglar, who served a long sentence, told the chaplain of the prison the following amusing story of one of his experiences: "One of the toughest pieces of work I undertook was a big jewelry shop in the Seven Sisters Road, one January night. It was a 'put up' job—that is, the business came to me through one of the brokers who supply burglars with places for likely hauls, and receive in return a large commission. The jewelry store in this case was protected by iron shutters, not easy to open from the street, but valuable goods were supposed to be left overnight in the window.

"I approached the crib down a narrow entry to the rear, and along this I walked backward, for the ground was covered with snow, and any tracks going forward would attract the next policeman who should pass. I continued on this crab-like progress until under the shutter of the rear window. This I got through without difficulty, but was confronted by a door leading into the passage, which was locked. On attempting to force it with a jimmy, the door fell together with its case with a tremendous crash. I need not say I made myself scarce in a jiffy, and hid behind a shed in the yard. Strange to say, nothing happened. No one seemed to have heard the terrible racket. I re-entered, and, climbing to the top of the stairs, found a heavy trapdoor fastened with a massive bolt. This gave way after a special treatment, and in the big sitting room, by the glimmer of my tiny dark lantern, I found a few watches. The door leading into the shop was fastened with a mortise lock, and it was necessary to cut the box out. Much to my disgust, I found the show-window absolutely empty. In ransacking the place, I came across a small iron safe which, with a vast deal of trouble, I dragged into the basement, where I set to work with my safe-opening tools, feeling sure I should find my plunder, but again I was disappointed, for the safe was empty." (Almost all English safes are key-locked, not combination as in America.)

"Where was the stuff? Clearly the jeweler had some hiding-place. I resolved not to get 'cold feet' on this job, so went back to make a systematic search. Outside the old couple's bedroom, I listened carefully. All was quiet. I entered as silently as a shadow, and found the old jeweler and his wife sleeping soundly. A revolver was on the chair by his bedside. I have always considered the practise of keeping revolvers about the house most dangerous, especially to casual night visitors, so I pocketed this one, gathered up the loose money, two gold watches, and, turning, found arranged along the wall, the rods of jewelry and watches from the shop window. I selected as many as my pockets would hold, and cautiously made my way downstairs again. Upon leaving the house, I walked backward again through the snow, and almost collided with the milkman just starting on his rounds.

"'You have a very remarkable way of walking,' he said.

"'Oh,' I replied, 'it is an agreeable change after the monotony of always walking forward; but in the daytime I cannot practise it, owing to the remarks of foolish people who will not mind their own business.'

"He seemed to enter into the joke, but no sooner had we reached the road, than he shouted, 'Police!' and 'Stop thief!' for all he was worth.

"I had a good start, however, and two hours later a Hoxton 'fence' received a considerable addition to his store of valuables concealed under the floor of his bedroom."

The question has often been asked how burglars get away with their booty, especially when it makes, as it often does, a bulky bundle. The police are apt to be suspicious of people who carry bundles in the small hours of the night, and ask inconvenient questions. If any one doubts this, let him try the experiment of going out between two and three in the morning, carrying a bag heavily loaded with bricks. He will not proceed many yards without being pounced upon by a "cop." A story in point is told by an ex-convict to a well-known detective:

"I had a pal with me, and we broke into the country palace of one of the wealthiest dukes in England. The silver-plate we got filled two bags. We had just dragged the sacks into the thicket near the house when the alarm was raised. Think of the tight place we were in—two o'clock in the morning, and a policeman every thirty yards all around the grounds, every road guarded and every path. Safe enough inside the ring we were, but when daylight came, what would happen? Still the next day dawned, and no trace was found either of the plunder, or of us, and by evening of that same day, it was all melted and sold to the 'fence' in the city. The police were utterly baffled as to how the perpetrators of the robbery got away with two sacks full of plate. No one had passed the cordon of police except a couple of countrymen from the home farm, who were driving a cart to market, containing a slaughtered sheep. Now I might tell the police something that would interest them. If they had turned that sheep over, they would have found, instead of the usual bodily organs, that the carcass contained a valuable collection of silver, and if they had looked under the straw, they might have found the rest of the duke's missing property."

The Second-Story Man. The professional burglar of standing in his profession looks down somewhat with condescension upon the second-story burglar, whose risks are not nearly so great, and whose rewards, of course, are proportionately smaller. The second-story man avoids breaking and entering a house. His forte is obtaining an entrance by means of convenient porches, over-hanging boughs of trees, water-conductors, and lightning-rods, up which he climbs with the greatest ease, and enters through an unguarded window in that part of the house where he has planned to make his robbery.

Many successful second-story men work only in the daytime, and are prepared with all sorts of plausible excuses to explain their presence if detected in a house. A burglar engaged in going through the premises after jewels known to be in the house may, in a second's time, assume all the appearance and actions of the honest workman come to repair the plumbing, and by his clever effrontery, escape even after he is detected. Usually, however, the second-story man so plans and times his work as to enter the house when most of the family are absent, and thus avoid the risk of detection.

BURGLARS' SUPERSTITIONS

Some people imagine that a burglar is forever on the still hunt for plunder; that the breaking into houses forms a nightly part of his program, and that he would be a lonesome individual unless he had a dark lantern in one hand and a jimmy in the other. The truth of the matter is that professional burglars rarely make more than eight or ten good hauls in the course of a season, and that to be out on more than one job inside of a week or ten days would be considered rather dangerous. Of course, there are cases where gangs of burglars are working certain sections of the city where a number of startling robberies are committed one after another, but your careful and successful cracksman limits his work and increases his safety.

The burglar, no doubt, may be a quiet citizen, a householder himself, and one known as a respectable man to his neighbors, and when occasionally he disappears for a week or a fortnight, it is attributed to business in a distant city. His "business" brings him in another rich haul, and when that is disposed of he is on "Easy" street again until inclination or necessity compels him to go forth in quest of other plunder.

Sailors are superstitious, but burglars share that honor with them, for there is no class of individuals who look more carefully to signs of good and evil omen than does your professional crib cracker. From an ex-convict whom I once befriended, in Omaha, and from other sources, I learned the following most common superstitions of thieves and burglars.

A black cat is a certain forerunner of disaster to the burglar, and householders who suddenly find their black cats poisoned may take it as a warning that the robbery of their domain has been decided upon, for the criminals take care to destroy their dumb enemies before paying a midnight call. Dogs, on the contrary, they fear but little, however savage they may be, because they take care to carry in their pockets pieces of ivory, a certain cure for dog-bites.

The cries of an infant warn the marauder that misfortune awaits him in the neighborhood. He will not stay in a house if he finds a clock stopped, a broken mirror, or an unframed oil painting; these are infallible omens of disaster.

One of the chief terrors of the burglar is a newly painted house. Several years ago in a northern town, some disciples of the jimmy broke into a large domicile, but removed nothing, though they favored the next house with a visit the same evening and stole everything of value. They were captured as they were scaling the garden wall, and at the trial one confessed that they had spent eight weeks in making preparations for entering the house from which they removed nothing, and upon doing so found it to have been freshly painted, so transferred their attention to the adjoining building, thereby bringing about their capture.

A criminal studies the weather quite as carefully as the farmer does. He will not perpetrate a crime on the night of a new moon, nor if the orb has a halo or mist round it. And were he to plunder a house during an eclipse, he might as soon give himself up to the law at once, for his days outside of prison walls would be numbered. Even more trifling incidents are of equal significance to the robber. It is bad luck to be followed by a dog, and any undertaking or plundering plan will be abandoned for the time, as it means capture or failure.

If the house selected has crape on the door, to enter

would be to court disaster, and to kick against a piece of coal in the road would bring about a similar result.

Pickpockets are very careful not to rob a cross-eyed or club-footed person. To rob a blind man would be to bring down misfortune; but, curiously enough, a blind woman can be victimized with impunity. A stolen purse that contains a battered coin or lock of hair is thrown away intact, or the thief will find himself a prisoner before the day is out.

Talismans are freely carried and implicitly believed in. Burglars in the olden days used to rob a house by the light of a candle made of human fat; but the superstition has nearly died out, owing to the difficulty of procuring material to make them, although it is still prevalent to some extent in Scotland and Ireland. When Burke and Hare were murdering human beings for the medical profession in Scotland, in 1828, it is claimed they also supplied human fat to burglars, the doctors giving Hare a few bottles, as they were told it was a good cure for rheumatism. The medicos treated it as a joke, but Hare sold it to some of the housebreakers he was intimate with. Old nails, broken horseshoes, curiously shaped pebbles, and endless other trinkets have times without number been found in the pockets of captured criminals who have begged that everything else they possessed should be taken from them rather than the talisman to which they pinned their faith. Charles Peace—perhaps the greatest burglar who ever lived—said that his success was due to the pawn-ticket of a violin he pawned when he was a boy, and which he always carried with him.

THIEVES AND THEIR TRICKS

A thief is one who appropriates any kind of property or money to his own use without the consent of the owner. As distinguished from a burglar, a thief does not break into a house or enter in the nighttime, but takes his plunder wherever he can find it. A thief may gain entrance to a house and steal a valuable diamond, but he uses his sharp wits to pass the door instead of the burglars' jimmy and skeleton keys.

There are thieves of various kinds, from the common sneak thief and shoplifter to the expert pickpocket and clever swindler, who sometimes makes hauls amounting to many thousands of dollars. The use of the word "thief," however, is generally confined to such classes of criminals as shoplifters, pickpockets, and the like. Overcoat thieves ply their trade in the residential sections of the city. They will sometimes ring the front doorbell and ask for the master or mistress of the house, giving some plausible pretext, and usually the name of the party living there. While the servant has gone to tell the mistress of the caller, he quietly picks up what garments are in sight on the hat-rack and makes off with them.

The Venetian blind thief got his name from the practise of the English thieves of making the pretext that they had come to repair the blinds of the house. A thief will call at the door claiming to be a mechanic to look over the house for necessary repairs, and in his rounds will gather up any valuable article that he can lay his hands on. This class of rascal even impersonates the plumber or the gas inspector with equally successful results.

Thieves at church are a very common occurrence. A case is related in London not long ago where a chapel had been furnished with one hundred new Bibles. They were first used at the afternoon service, and when the congregation gathered for evening they had all disappeared. A very common experience of church officers is to find that books disappear gradually; not only books but also hassocks and cushions are taken from houses of worship. Petty robberies from the collection box are not infrequent. In some localities the custom of covering one's offering with one's hand so that other worshipers shall not see the amount given gives the thief his opportunity, for in the rapid passing of the plate it is easy for the skillful professional thief to put in a penny and at the same moment take out a dollar. This is sometimes done by a sticky substance put upon a single finger. Umbrella thieves and pickpockets also ply their trade in church as well as in other places of public gathering.

'How can you detect a church thief?' is a question I have often asked detectives. There seems to be no real answer; but, as a general rule, it is just as well to look out for your property as carefully when you are in church as when you are out.

Thieves as Wedding Guests. There is scarcely a fashionable wedding where the contracting parties are wealthy that does not suffer from the presence of wedding thieves. For this reason, the more expensive terns of jewelry are often imitated in paste before they are put on exhibition among the gifts, while the originals are sent to the bank. The wedding gift lifter works his game as follows: Disguised as a tradesman or assistant, he gains the confidence of the servants, gets a description of a diamond tiara, or other article of great value, which he then has a duplicate made of set with imitation paste diamonds. He will even go as far as to pay $15 or $100 for a good imitation article. Armed with this and perfectly dressed, he makes his way among the party of guests and finds it no great risk to adroitly change the counterfeit for the genuine jewel.

Trick of the Van Thief. Vans that are covered entirely with tarpaulin or canvas and have a loose back present opportunities to the van thief. A favorite trick is for the thief to wheel a hand-cart, covered with sacking, under which a confederate lies concealed, behind one of these vans. The confederate quickly puts the upper part of his body inside the van, his feet remaining in the cart. Being concealed from view by the loose tarpaulin, he seizes a package, dropping back with it into the cart, which is pushed off at once. A wet day is preferred for this trick, as then not so many people are about, and the driver is likely to be holding his head down as a protection from the rain, in consequence of which he will not look behind.

The Trick Satchel Thieves. It is when the dark days come round that the railway-station thief most safely conducts his operations. The summer tourist he loves not, for his luggage contains few valuables, and there is then too much light about. A dull afternoon and well-to-do people going off by train are what the platform prowler asks for. And here is shown as a warning, if needs be, an artful appliance that station thieves have used of late years. It looks like an ordinary portmanteau; and so it is with a difference.

It is a specially made portmanteau, the bottom of

which closes up on pressure being applied. Thus when the "trick" portmanteau is placed over a smaller one that lies upon the platform, the larger one comes down as a cover over it. By a movement of the thumb of the hand that holds the portmanteau handle, powerful springs are released which tightly grasp the portmanteau that is inside, and it can thus be carried away completely enveloped from sight.

If, therefore, you see a suspicious-looking character hanging about, don't set him down as a genuine passenger just because he has a bag.

Diamond in a Chew of Gum. One of the cleverest and most unscrupulous diamond thieves I ever heard of perfected a scheme for daylight robbery of unmounted gems which for a time simply defied detectives of London and Paris. The game was played as follows:

A lady, well dressed and looking like a respectable and wealthy matron who might be the wife of a banker or large merchant, enters a jewelry store and asks to see some unmounted diamonds. The clerk shows her the stones, and while she is looking at them, a second lady equally respectable in appearance enters and approaches the same counter. She seems to be interested in diamonds. Suddenly one of the most valuable gems is missing. The proprietor is summoned, the detectives rush in, and an officer is called. The women, who both declare their innocence, are carefully searched, but the diamond has absolutely disappeared. Eventually both the women are released, but the diamond is never recovered.

The way the trick was played is this:

One of the women (both of whom are members of the gang) deftly concealed the diamond in a piece of chewing gum and sticks it on the under side of the front edge of the counter.

There it remains safely hidden away while the frantic search is going on. A third member of the gang slips in afterward with the crowd of curious and removes the gum containing the diamond and makes off with it.

THE ARISTOCRAT OF THIEVERY

There are kings of crime as well as kings of finance. Much the same talent that enables John D. Rockefeller to pile up a thousand million dollars or Henry H. Rogers to control unnumbered millions in Wall Street, applied in a different direction, develops that high grade of criminal whose robberies are exploited in scare-head stories in newspapers, and are the talk of the country for many days. The case which occurred at Liverpool a short time ago was the work of a bright man. The circumstances related to me by a newspaper man are as follows: "One day Messrs. Oldfield & Co., of Liverpool, received a telegram purporting to come from Mrs. Brattlebank, of Garston, then staying in London, ordering a quantity of diamonds to be sent to her Garston residence. Mrs. Brattlebank being a wealthy customer and well known to this jewelry house, a package of valuable stones was made up and sent by registered post, after being insured for $5,000.

"After the arrival of the package in Garston, a well-dressed gentleman representing himself to be Mr. Laing Miller, a wealthy South African ship owner and a friend of the Brattlebanks, called at the residence, having previously explained by telephone that he was coming to take the package to Mrs. Brattlebank in London. The whole affair seemed so open and aboveboard, and the appearance of Mr. Miller so honest and convincing, that the valuable package was handed over to him without question. Neither Mr. Miller, who is now suspected to be one of the most expert confidence men in the Kingdom, nor the diamonds have ever been seen since."

The Swindler Who Lowered a Check. The crime of raising a check is often attempted, and sometimes successfully, but it is seldom that a criminal attempts to lower the figures on a check and cash it for a less sum than it was made out for. The following incident occurred in Wall Street not long ago, showing that the man who conceived it must have had a ready wit and a clever brain, as well as considerable daring to put it into execution. It is said that this ingenious swindler had already realized between two and three thousand dollars by his startling new method of lowering checks.

For instance, a stock exchange broker sells one thousand shares of a stock to ten customers in blocks of one hundred shares at 91. Each purchaser prepares a check for $9,100 for the seller when the messenger boys make their rounds. If the checks are not ready when the messenger calls out to the cashier, who usually cannot see the boy, he is told to come back later.

This swindler follows a messenger boy, and when the boy is told to return later the fellow returns himself in a short time and gets the check, which is readily handed over to him.

Having secured the check for $9,100 the swindler hurries away, and, knowing that safety does not lie in presenting the check for so large an amount, reduces it to $910, makes it payable to bearer by the use of chemicals, and secures the money.

A Daring Train Robbery. Among the clever coups that have come to my attention here is one related by an ex-convict, and published recently in an English periodical that presents some rather interesting features. The writer says: "A certain lady of high social position was known to possess an exceptionally valuable collection of jewelry, and some of us had long been casting covetous eyes upon it. One day she started from St. Pancras in the Scotch express for her husband's seat in the Highlands, the jewelry being securely packed in one of her numerous trunks. These were duly placed in the luggage van, which was locked, and only opened by the guard at the two or three places where the express stopped. No one save the railway servants entered the van or left it, neither had the doors been opened while the train was in motion. But when the trunk in question was unlocked far away in Scotland, the jewel case was gone, and from that day to this not the slightest clue has been found as to its disappearance. Here was a case for a Sherlock Holmes or a Martin Hewitt, but either these gentlemen were not forthcoming, or they totally failed to solve what is, perhaps, the most mysterious railway robbery of recent days.

"Let me lift the veil and show how the little job was worked. Two men, both of whom are still making a very comfortable income as railway thieves, got to know of the lady's proposed journey, and discovered the train by which she intended to travel. Accordingly, they also traveled north by that train, though they did not go as far as Scotland. On the contrary, they only booked to

Leeds. Their luggage consisted of two portmanteaus and a massive wooden trunk, strongly hooped and pad-locked. It was an honest, straightforward-looking trunk, but any one who examined it very closely might have discovered a quantity of small holes in its sides, practically concealed by the iron hoops, between which and the woodwork there was at intervals a slight space. That trunk did not contain the large assortment of wearing apparel that might have been supposed; in fact, it only contained one suit of clothes, and that suit encased the limbs of a boy of fourteen!

"As soon as the train was well on its journey, one end of the trunk opened, and the small boy emerged. With the aid of a goodly stock of skeleton keys and pick-locks—the English hamper locks can be opened with a button-hook, they are so simple—he opened the various hampers bearing her ladyship's name, and presently discovered the jewel case, which he removed to his own box. He then locked up the trunks, returned to his hiding-place, closed the sliding panel, curled himself up comfortably in the box, and went to sleep for the rest of the journey.

"At Leeds the two men alighted, called a porter, who got their luggage out of the van for them, and then drove in a cab to a certain temperance hotel in Briggate, where, in the privacy of the room they had secured, the boy was let out of the box, and the jewel case gleefully examined. Its contents traveled back to London by the next train, and were safely on the continent before the news of the robbery had reached Scotland Yard."

A Check for $30,000. A single "plant" on a Chicago

bank was pulled off recently, whereby the clever swindler coppered out $30,000 for himself with very little effort. The bank officers tried to hush the matter up as much as possible, and for the sake of the depositors I shall not give the name of the institution, but the facts of which I am certain are substantially as follows: A depositor of several years' standing appeared a few days ago in the bank president's office with a draft on London for £6,000, which was perfectly good. The depositor informed the president he desired to deposit this London draft, and at the same time to check against it, presenting his check for $30,000 for the president to OK.

The latter put his initials on it and thought no more of the transaction. The depositor then went out into the bank and deposited his London draft, and on the following day presented a check for $30,000, which was paid, the teller knowing that that amount was to his credit on the books. Later in the day he again appeared at the window and presented the check for $30,000, which had been initialed by the president. This check was also paid. Nothing more has since been seen of the depositor.

PICKPOCKETS AT WORK

Among the most interesting classes of thieves is the pickpocket, whose clever subterfuges and skill of hand have been so often exploited in novel and storybook. Your professional pickpocket is naturally a rover, and travels the country over, attending large gatherings. Of professional pickpockets there are a number of types, each adapted to the class of "work" in which he engages.

It is the usual opinion that a pickpocket is a forbidding and suspicious looking fellow, but a glance at the rogues' gallery in any police headquarters will show you that they look much like ordinary individuals, and are of more than average intelligence. The pickpocket is usually very well dressed and of prepossessing appearance. Those who seek to make only large hauls are entertaining talkers and easy in their manner. They are generally self-possessed and, while dexterous, are very cautious in their operations.

It is needless to say that women make the most patient as well as the most dangerous pickpockets. It is simply amazing how quickly an expert pickpocket, with a delicate touch, seemingly accidental, will locate the resting-place of a well-filled purse or other article of value that he chooses to abstract. When once discovered they follow their intended victims until the proper opportunity comes. A common pickpocket trick is for the operator to carry a shawl or overcoat carelessly over the left arm, and to take a seat on the right side of the person they intend to rob in a streetcar or other vehicle.

Sometimes a small and very sharp knife is used to cut the side of the dress or pantaloons of the victim, so that the purse may be abstracted without going into the pocket directly. Others of this light-fingered gentry wear light overcoats with large pockets removed. They will endeavor to stand near a person, preferably a woman, who is paying her fare and has displayed a well-filled purse. The pickpocket then carelessly throws his coat over her dress, and by inserting his hand through the outside opening of his own pocket, quietly proceeds to abstract her purse. Pickpockets either work alone or in pairs, or what is called a mob. Most female pickpockets seem to prefer to work alone, sometimes, however, working in conjunction with a man thief to whom they pass their plunder, and thus make detection impossible if they are suspected and searched.

The mob is a gang of expert pickpockets under the direction of a leader who has had experience, and knows all the tricks. Their usual game is to frequent some crowded platform or a railway station, and raise an apparent row in which two men seem to engage in a scuffle or quarrel and come to blows. Others rush in attempting to separate them, and the attention of the whole crowd of people is for the moment directed strongly that way. At the same moment other single light-fingered members of the same gang crowd in with the citizens who are being jostled, and abstract their pocketbooks and watches without any trouble. Recently a gang has successfully worked in several of the subway stations in Boston, and the same gang has successfully plied this vocation in New York, Chicago, and Philadelphia.

The false-arm game, or the "third mit," as it is known to the professional pickpocket, is said to be little employed in this country now. A loose cape overcoat is worn in one of the sleeves of which a false arm and hand are fixed. Thus a detective who may be watching the pickpocket will see apparently both of his hands in view, while in reality the light skillful fingers of the operator's left hand are going through the pockets of the man beside of whom he is standing. This dodge is very much employed on the continent by shoplifters.

One of the many fertile dodges by which a pickpocket escapes detection is known as the horse-dodge. The thief so arranges as to meet his victim by the side of a horse standing by the curbstone. He has previously located the watch or purse he wishes to lift, and with a quick blow he knocks his victim's hat over his eyes, grabs the pocketbook or watch or whatever else he is after, and immediately darts under the horse, and hides himself in the traffic on the other side. By the time the victim has got the use of his eyes, and is able to look around, the thief has entirely disappeared, and he would not be apt to look in the right direction, at any rate.

In the outskirts of London, among the small shops, a rather unusual trick has been played frequently upon unsuspecting shopkeepers. Two men in earnest argument over some matter enter a small grocery store and approach the proprietor who is behind his till. One man says to the proprietor, "My friend and I have gottten into an argument over a peculiar matter which we believe you can settle for us. I have bet him that my hat," taking off an old-fashioned stove-pipe hat, "will hold more than four quarts of molasses, while he contends that it will hold hardly three quarts. We are willing to buy the molasses if you will fill this hat and prove the question to decide the bet." The shopkeeper good-humoredly agrees, and brings the hat brimful with sticky molasses, at which one of the thieves slaps it over the shopkeeper's head, and before he can extricate himself and call help they have robbed the till and disappeared.

BEGGING LETTER SWINDLES

Every section of the country, almost every city, has one or more begging letter writers, who ply their trade with greater or less success, and exercise their arts upon the simple and credulous. These clever rascals range all the way from the ignorant crook that writes a pitiful story of want and misery, and who neither receives nor expects more than a few dollars at a time, to the master of the craft, who goes about it like a regular business, has a well-organized office and a force of stenographers and clerks, who are kept busy day in and day out sending off and receiving mail.

Several remarkable cases have been unearthed only lately, where the fake was receiving hundreds of letters daily, the large majority of them containing money. The post-office authorities, however, have been getting after this class of rogues very sharply of late, and any organized plundering by the use of the mails, is almost certain to come to an untimely end sooner or later.

If any one has reason to believe that a business of the kind is conducted on fraudulent lines, a complaint to one of the post-office inspectors in any large city will quickly bring a "fraud order" against the party, restraining them from use of the mails, and a rigid investigation follows. Then the game is up, and it's back to the "tall timber" for them. It is a well-known fact, however, that this recourse to the "fraud order" is frequently used by unprincipled persons, out of spite and to obtain revenge upon those who are actually conducting a legitimate business. The fraudulent advertisement is often an adjunct to the bogus letter scheme, and designed to get names to whom a special kind of letter may be written. One of the most daring schemes of this kind was unearthed a short time ago in New York City. A man fitted up a suite of offices in elegant style in one of the large office buildings. He then traveled to South Dakota, and under the laws of that State, incorporated a stock company, with a capitalization of five million dollars. It was called a commercial and mining company. Returning to New York, he instructed the Press Clipping Bureau to save him the obituary notices of all males that died in the States other than New York—just far enough away from the center of operations to be comfortable for him.

Using these obituary notices for guides, he would, write to the dead man, notifying him that the last payment was due on the five hundred or one thousand shares of stock which he had bought at fifty cents a share. He congratulated the man on his foresight on investing in this stock, as it had gone up several points, and was still rising in value. He begged that a remittance in final payment of this stock should be sent at once.

A beautifully engrossed certificate of stock was enclosed in the letter to the dead man, and the inevitable result was that the surviving relatives, thinking the departed one had bought this stock quietly and forgotten to mention it, sent on a check for all the way from five hundred to one hundred dollars as requested. It was one of the prettiest schemes that has been worked for a long time, and the actual amount of money realized by the swindler will never be known. Such a "snap" could not last long, however, and the promulgator of the swindle was soon detected and brought to trial.

One man advertised to sell ten yards of good silk for twenty-five cents, and so worded his announcement as to suggest a bankrupt sale or smuggled goods. For a time he reaped a rich harvest. Money came thick and fast. To each of his dupes he mailed ten yards of sewing silk.

Another rascal offered a complete and perfect sewing machine for one dollar. He, also, gathered in the dollars at a rapid rate, till Uncle Sam put a stop to his operations—he sent his victims a common sewing needle.

This is quite in line with the fellow who advertised a few years ago to tell a sure way of getting rid of chinch bugs for one dollar. After the victim had sent the dollar, he received by mail a card upon which was printed the following:

Catch the chinch bug. Hold it by the legs carefully between the thumb and forefinger. Lay its head on the anvil, and hit it with a hammer as hard as you can.

Many of these advertisements are inserted merely to receive names and addresses of credulous people. The lists of names are then sold or rented out to fake mail-order houses, who proceed to circularize them.

Chain letter schemes are now declared illegal, but for some time a number of clever dodges of this kind were worked throughout the United States as well as on the continent. A brief description of one of these schemes will show the character of this kind of enterprise:

The scheme was where a trip to the Paris Exposition, with two hundred dollars for expenses, was offered as a prize. Each person entering the contest was required to

pay thirty cents, then send to friends two letters, request-
ing them to send their names to the original promoter,
and send duplicate letters to two of their friends, the op-
eration to be repeated indefinitely.

Each person writing to the original promoter was to
receive an offer, allowing him to start a chain on his own
account, on payment of thirty cents, the trip and money
going to the one whose chain brings out the largest number of letters. The ostensible object was to secure names
for employment at the exposition.

TRICKS OF BUNCO MEN

Something for nothing has ever tempted the simple and
unsophisticated; indeed, it is a trait of human nature
upon which the swindler everywhere, and in all ages, has
relied to his profit.

The origin of the term "bunco" comes from an old
English game of chance in which a checkered cloth covered with numbers and stars is covered with a hood called
a "bunco." The game was to throw dice that counted up
to a certain concealed number. The man who knew the
game was called the "bunco man," or the banker, and
later when this form of swindle became notorious the
term was corrupted into "bunco." Today the word is used
to denote almost any swindle where the victim is made to
believe he is to receive a large sum of money or valuables,
and then gets nothing at all.

The real Simon Pure Bunco Game, as practiced in the
United States some years ago by Tom O'Brien, the King

of Bunco Men, was played as follows: The victim, some wealthy farmer usually, was lured to a room at a hotel and a game was proposed. A confederate took the part of another player. A pack of forty-eight cards in eight sets, each set numbered from one to six was produced, shuffled, and dealt out eight cards to each player. The total sum of the numbers in each hand was then compared with the number carrying a prize on the chart. If it corresponded, the hand won the prize.

The cards are gravely counted and compared. The dealer then says to the con federate and dupe:

"Gentlemen, you have drawn the grand conditional advertising prize. You're entitled to $10,000 apiece on condition that you prove yourselves worth $50,000, and promise to advertise our battery, whether you win or lose. You will have to put up $10,000 apiece against the $10,000 prize; then you draw once more. If you draw a star number you get only the $10,000 prize and your money back. If you draw any other number you get its prize added to your own money and the big prize."

The confederate says he is worth more than $50,000 and declares his intention of going and getting the $10,000 stake. The dupe is also persuaded to put up the cash and both winners go away to get the money. They return and the money is put up. Four cards are dealt each. The total of each hand is twenty-eight.

"Why, gentlemen," says the bunco man in apparent surprise, "twenty-eight is the 'State number,' the total blank! You have lost all!"

The confederate pretends to be very much broken up, condones, with his "fellow victim" and gets him out of the room as soon as he can. In a few moments he gives the farmer the slip, joins his partner, and they escape from town as quickly as possible.

Such is the principle of the bunco game, and it is worked under many guises with cards, dice, at the pool or billiard table—our pool-room bunco is known as *"selling the lemon"* as bets are made on the yellow ball—but always with the idea of making the victim believe he is going to get something for nothing.

A variation of the bunco game, often played in the farming districts, is for a well-dressed, plausible man to drive up to a well-to-do farmer's home and inquire if he knows of a good farm for sale. If he does, he is invited to drive with the stranger to take a look at it and give his advice. The farmer finds his new acquaintance bright and entertaining. The property is reached and the sharper with apparent satisfaction inspects the land and buildings, and closes a bargain without much haggling. In the course of conversation the man from the city flashes a big roll of bank notes of high denomination and the farmer is duly impressed.

As they drive homeward a confederate will appear who stops the carriage to make some inquiry. The three enter into conversation and good-natured chaffing leads up to a proposal of some game of cards or bet. The farmer is induced to take a hand, the first swindler offering to put up his half of the stake. When the two "partners"— the farmer and the first swindler—have won a large sum the loser asks for proof of their ability to make good their stake. The first swindler produces the cash, and the farmer drives with him to the next town to draw his money out of the bank to make good his claim.

Now comes the rapid denouncement. The first

swindler asks the farmer to oblige him by taking charge of all the money, including the money with which he is to buy the farm, until he can return and close the bargain. The countryman, naturally pleased at this confidence, is induced to put his own money in the same convenient tin box which the stranger has ready. At that point the stranger and the farmer part. The former to parts unknown, the latter with his precious tin box under his arm, and when he gets home he finds, instead of money, that the box is filled only with heavy folded papers to give it the same weight. A rapid shift has been made before his eyes without his detecting it; his money is gone, and two adroit scoundrels are far away.

Among the most famous (or infamous) bunco men of this country are Tom O'Brien, mentioned above, William Raymond, "Doc" Mincheon, George Post, William Barracks, Lewis Ludlow, and Clay Wilson. O'Brien is serving a life sentence for murder, but Post is supposed to be still at his old tricks.

Jacob Sindheim, alias "Al" Wise, has a star game. His lay is to persuade a gullible person that he has a secret process by means of which genuine gold coins can be "sweated" or robbed of a portion of their gold, by a certain solution, without impairing their appearance. Several times he has induced speculative individuals without conscience, to construct tanks in the basement of their houses and put in from $10,000 to $20,000 in gold pieces for treatment. Twenty days are to be required for the process. Before that time he removes all the gold, which it is needless to say has lost not a grain of its weight, and makes his escape. The victim, after getting tired of waiting, opens the tank to find a liberal deposit of paving-stones instead of gold coins. Then he wakes up.

If men did not try and get something for nothing they might often be able to retain that which they have.

One of the latest dodges of a bunco nature is a bogus express company which caters to those who never receive packages by express, but who want to. In a large room above its showy office a force of skilled workmen are employed, manufacturing bundles and filling them with old bricks and newspapers.

The express company, having made up a convincing-looking parcel, sends out a postal card to its prospective victim on which it says:

MR. E. Z. MARK STEINER, 398 JAY STREET:

Please furnish us with your address, as there is a package addressed to you at our office.

COMEANDGO EXPRESS CO.

The fact that the express company has written to him at his address to ask him what his address is does not strike the victim as strange. The "company" does it in order that it may get in writing from Mr. Steiner a request to deliver the package, thus making him its debtor to the extent of the "express charges," usually $2.

THE GAME OF WITS

When the corn-husking is over and the county fairs begin their annual three and four-day sessions in a thousand agricultural centers, a silent army of confidence men and swindlers make ready for their richest harvest of the year! The county fairs are rich fields for their particular work, and they intend to make the most of their opportunities.

The three-shell-game man has been a feature of such gatherings from time immemorial. The game in some form or other has been played ever since Rome was founded. Three half walnut shells or metal covers are used and a small and exceedingly lively pea made of soft rubber. The gaping yokel is invited to pick the shell under which the " pea" reposes. The clever manipulator tosses it from one to another, then, with an apparent awkward twist, seems to throw it under a certain one. The rustic backs his opinion with his coin. The shells are lifted. The former was mistaken and pays for his experience.

It is only another case of where the manipulation of the hand deceives the eye. They say that a new "sucker" is born every minute. Certain it is that this old game finds its dupes as plentiful as in the days of our grandfathers. The callow youth of today is willing to bet his last cent that he can put his finger on the shell that covers the "pea" for he has seen it put there!

But if the unsuspecting countryman is an easy mark for cheats at his county fairs, he is often even more "accessible" when he comes to the city. The following story from the New York *Telegraph* is especially good on account of its breezy style and true-to-life description of the methods of the quick-witted gentry. The story is entitled:

Was Kind To Strangers

Oh, the shame of it, that S. G. Dabdoub of Jersey

City should journey all the way from his native heath to Boston and there accept bad money from a stranger!

Hideous circumstance! Malicious fate! If there is a Mrs. Dabdoub, what will she say?

Dabdoub! The very name smacks of caution.

But when he reached Boston and saw all the houses, and still was gazing upon them from his point of vantage at the railroad station, a stranger who had been peering furtively from the dense underbrush observed him.

After retiring behind a freight-car and throwing a few joyous hand-springs, as if pleased at something, the stranger muttered:

"He will do. I have not waited in vain. Tonight in my palatial residence there shall be joy and feasting and seeming laughter. Ah! It is good to live!"

After this mysterious and ingrowing conversation, sometimes yclept monologue, the stranger dashed up to Mr. Dabdoub, of far Jersey, and said in his panting tone of a man who had gone seven furlongs under the spur of cruel circumstances: "Can you give me change for a fifty dollar bill?"

Mr. Dabdoub could, would, and did, and the stranger, without stopping to count the money, placed a bill in the Jersey man's hands, expressed his thanks in a monosyllable, and hurried away.

Horrors! The bill he left behind was a Confederate one.

Mr. Dabdoub, incensed, pursued, but the stranger wore the seven league boots of successful guilt, and it is unlikely that Nick Carter could have caught him.

Dabdoub went to the police, who wept with him and addressed him as if he had been a public meeting.

Here is another adroit swindle that might almost be considered better than a gold brick.

Some time ago a young fellow with a violin under his arm entered a market-place in one of our large cities, made his purchase, and then found himself short of money. However, he offered the fiddle as security, while he fetched the necessary amount of cash. Scarcely had he left the place when a well-dressed man entered and saw the fiddle on the counter. He examined it and cried out that it was a Stradivarius.

"Why, I'll give you $300 for it," he said. The shopkeeper refused to sell it without consulting the owner, and the second stranger went away leaving five dollars for the refusal of the treasure. Presently, the first rogue returned, was informed of the offer, and said he would agree, providing the tradesman would give him $150 down. The victim complied, and neither of the swindlers ever returned. The fiddle was worth about $1.50.

But don't get the idea that farmers and small shopkeepers are the only prey of the bunco man, the swindler and the confidence man. A city man on a farm the first time and trying to run it, is of a greener green than a farmer in a city buying gold bricks. Here are some games successfully played on the dwellers in cities.

THE CLEVER "SOFA GAME"

Of all the men who live by their wits, the English crook who conceived and carried into successful execution the so-called "sofa game" certainly deserves the palm. So ingenious, so daring, and yet so simple, is this scheme that it deserves a special description. The reader will notice that it partakes both of the nature of a confidence game and a first-class burglary job.

The game requires the cooperation of several members of a gang, one of whom must be a boy or a young man of small stature and slender physique. Sometimes a young woman is employed, who, if discovered, throws herself upon the mercy of the householder. The gang first selects the residence of some wealthy citizen. If inside information about the silver and jewels to be looted can be secured, so much the better. The habits of the members of the family are closely observed and then at an hour when the fewest possible people are at home the plan is put into execution.

This is what happens:

A furniture wagon drives up to the house and a well-dressed man of respectable appearance and plausible address rings the front-door bell. The door is opened, the following conversation ensues:

"Is this the residence of Mr. John Rahner?"

"Yes, but Mr. Rahner is not at home."

"Dear, dear, that is unfortunate! But, however, it does not matter. I have been commissioned as chairman of a committee of the Dearborn Lodge (naming some order to which the householder actually belongs) to present

Mr. Rahner with this beautiful sofa (indicating an imposing piece of furniture on the wagon). Shall my men bring it in?"

"Why, yes, if you are sure this is the right place."

"No mistake about that, Madam; Mr. Rahner is greatly esteemed by the members of the lodge and this gift is to be a complete surprise!"

So in the sofa is carried and deposited in a place of honor in the drawing-room. The polite "lodge member" depreciating all thanks departs and the team drives away.

A few hours later the polite stranger reappears in hot haste and the wagon drives up again. He is profuse in his apologies, but an error has been made.

"So unfortunate! So sorry to inconvenience you, but do you know I have made such a stupid blunder about the address—the sofa is to go to Brother John Rahner, of South Main Street, instead of North Main Street. Would it be too much bother to allow my men to enter and take it away? We are very anxious to deliver it before Brother Rahner returns, as it is a surprise for him!"

Of course, there is nothing to be done but let the beautiful sofa go, and, amid the apologies and excuses of the polite stranger, the sofa is again carried forth to the wagon and is driven away. The polite stranger also disappears, and, it is needless to say, is seen no more in that part of the town.

The next act on the program is the startling discovery that the house has been robbed of, perhaps, many thousands of dollars' worth of jewels and silver. How was it done?

The explanation is very simple. The sofa is specially constructed with a hollow compartment of considerable size. Inside a girl has been concealed, who, when the sofa is left alone, quietly comes out and ransacks the place and retreats with her plunder into this convenient hiding-place. Girl, plunder, and sofa are then all carried away together and the thieves make good their escape without delay.

This is a new game, and, as I say, has been worked with many variations and usually with success in almost every city in England and on the continent.

FAKE! FAKE! FAKE!

There are certain classes of men, and women, too, who, while not actually criminal, are yet so close to the boundary line in their practices as to need some special mention in this book. Take, for instance, the many so-called "divine" or mental healers, who pretend to cure all sorts of diseases by the laying on of hands or simply absent treatment, or the old-style patent medicine fraud who retailed sweetened and colored water under some high-sounding name, as Dr. So and So's Elixir and Tonic, from the tail-end of a cart, after having attracted a crowd of the curious with a lecture or open-air minstrel show.

"Far be it for me" to decry the actual healing and curative value of many excellent proprietary medicines and preparations on the market today. But among the good there are many that are worthless, and I should advise my readers to take such "remedies" only on the advice of their family physician.

The fake "doctor" is still with us, and his advertisements are often to be seen in the newspapers of America.

They usually advertise under some honest-sounding name, and assume all the titles and learned degrees of two continents. Some are actually physicians, and, failing in the regular practice, have set out to make a living by deluding suffering humanity. It would be amusing, if it were not sorrowful, to see the crowds of patients who bring their ailments to such "doctors." The game is to give the sufferer some relief at first, in order to encourage him, and then prolong his case through many weary weeks and months, until they have gotten all the money he can afford to spend. Such doctors usually call themselves "specialists," but their real specialty is in extorting money from their dupes, and my advice is to keep as far away from them as possible.

Thanks to the energetic efforts of the authorities many, if not all, of these practitioners have been driven out, and it is to be hoped that such tragedies as that unearthed in the Susan Geary case will be rare in the future.

The case of Francis Truth, alias Will Bemis, the self-styled Divine Healer, attracted no little attention throughout the East, especially in Boston, a few years ago. The man was a handsome, plausible, smooth-spoken man, who claimed to have some mysterious mesmeric power by which he could cure any disease, simply by the laying on of hands. His advertisements bristled with testimonials and brilliant promises, and he did a good business among the credulous. Many, who doubtless had nothing whatever the matter with them, were hypnotized into the belief that they were cured.

Finally, Truth—or Bemis—found his money getting limited, because he could only "treat" a limited number a day. Then he had recourse to the absent treatment dodge.

He would tell his patients that he would give them an absent treatment at a certain hour, and at that time they were to retire to their rooms and think of him, and they would receive the healing influence! As the number of his dupes grew, he branched into a mail-order feature, until hundreds and thousands of people who had never seen the "healer" were sending him money by mail. He received hundreds of letters each day, until the post-office was forced to deliver them in great bags, and his income amounted to thousands of dollars a week! Truth lived in great style, drove about in his own carriage, had quite an office force of stenographers and clerks to handle the mail, and was getting rich, hand over fist, when the post-office authorities and the police put an end to his career.

Advertising mediums, clairvoyants, and astrologers have hosts of dupes, and some invite the methods of the confidence man, with mystical advice and fortune-telling. Not long ago, a certain Miss Ethel L, of Maiden, Mass., visited a so-called medium in Boston. As soon as she entered his inner sanctum she was surprised to have him caution her about a large sum of money which she was carrying. This "occult" knowledge so inspired her confidence, that she asked his advice about a suit she was interested in. He told her he would have to put her in a trance, which he did. When she came out of it, he cautioned her to go directly home, and to *hold her fingers crossed* until she reached her own room, where she must remain for two days. It was actually some hours before she realized that she had been robbed of $1,000 which she had in her pocket. Of course, the medium had disappeared.

I must say that with all its boasted culture and

learning, Boston seems to be a favorite city for all sorts of schemes of this kind; astrologers, mediums, clairvoyants, test-mediums, and the like abound in the Hub as in few other places it has been my good fortune to visit, and I have been all over the world. Chicago also has its share.

New Yorkers pride themselves in believing in nothing at all, and yet it was only a short time ago that a man named Ridgley, and calling himself the East Indian Mystery, victimized many people of wealth and fashion in that metropolis. This remarkable person combined the fakir of the East with the modern magnetic healer and the Voodoo doctor of French Louisiana. The man himself is 70 years old. He is small, spry, alert, and wonderfully shrewd. His beard is bushy and black, except where age has whitened the edges, and grows thick and curly at the sides. The nose is as flat as a negro's. He denies negro blood, however, and abhors the race. He claims to be from Hindoostan, and talks to others in the house in a strange tongue.

The eyes of the man are small, shrewd, and dark. The forehead, from each side of which grows gray, bushy hair that hides the ears, is high, receding, and intelligent.

"I knew you were coming," says this wizard-like man, "and I determined to receive you though warned against you. Now you want to know what I am, what I do. Let us be honest with each other."

He chooses big words as he proceeds to describe himself. They are used aptly, but mispronounced. The "th" becomes "d," and there are other things not unfamiliar in the Southern negro. The East Indian proceeds to read your character and to tell you of your life. He does it well.

"I am not a fortune-teller," he explains. "They are

frauds, and I am a physiognomist. I read from the apex of the nose to the top of the forehead. I don't predict; I tell you; and I don't ask you to say if I am right or wrong."

It is said that among this man's patrons have been men and women whose names are a part of the life of New York.

It is also said that a recent marriage which astonished New York society came after the woman in the case had consulted this strange combination of charlatan and physician. She confided to him her desire, told him of her repeated failures to secure her wish, took the treatment, and in three months was married. Then followed, so the story goes, many presents, among them a tenement to the East Indian.

Spiritualism has many followers, and at one time I was almost a believer, but this was before I made a thorough investigation, which I have followed up even to the present day. I have never seen a materialization or a manifestation which I cannot fully explain. Of course, I cannot explain those that I "hear" about, as no two people see the same one thing alike.

Spiritualism is really a beautiful belief for those that are honest and believe in it; but as I have visited the greatest spiritualistic meetings in the world, I am sorry to say that no one has ever produced anything for me that would smack of the spiritual.

In Germany, spirit mediums are put in jail for obtaining money under false pretences. In England, Maskenlyne, of Maskenlyne & Cook, has done a great deal to keep the so-called fraud spiritualistic mediums out of England. In the future, I contemplate writing a book on spiritualistic methods, and how they do their tricks. I do not mean genuine spiritualists who have no tricks, but those mediums who use their knowledge of magic to gain a living.

The Davenport Brothers, during their short but strenuous career, had a terrible time of it in their journeys abroad. They were driven out of England, but they made enough money to last them the rest of their lives.

BOGUS TREASURES

Never believe that a so-called antique piece of furniture or a painting by one of the old masters is genuine until its authenticity has been proven beyond a possible doubt. That is my advice, and if you, reader, could see some of the impositions practised upon wealthy collectors and curio hunters, you, too, would take that view.

The people who purchase this class of goods are usually new-made millionaires, ambitious to own an art gallery of old masters. It would give them little satisfaction to know that some of their priceless treasures are simply copies, and often poor ones at that. M. Felix Duquesnel, of Paris, famous as an art critic, says that certain galleries of ancient masters contain few pictures more than ten years old. Forged pictures are regularly included in sales of private collections in which they never belonged. Nor is a written and duly attested pedigree of the least value. I know of one case in London where a dealer in fake antiques sought out an impoverished nobleman whose only property besides his title was an ancient manor house that was heavily mortgaged. The house was in a remote spot and had scarcely a stick of furniture left in it. The dealer bought it and sent out to it many vanloads of paintings, black oak furniture, arms, armour, moth-eaten tapestry, etc. In a few weeks he announced a sale of art treasures at the ancient home of the last of an ancient race. The sale actually lasted several weeks as though the very cellars had been packed with "art treasures."

On the continent, to my certain knowledge, the case is even worse. One man that began life as a sculptor's assistant, but soon began the manufacture of imitations of "ancient" statues and "antique" furniture, now makes about $7,500 a year and employs several workmen.

His masterpieces are certain Greek heads "attributed to Phidias" but he also makes eighteenth century and Empire furniture. The opinion of such an authority is valuable. He says: "You can take it as a fact that even an art expert can no longer tell if a piece of furniture is a forgery. At least, yes, he can tell if he takes the furniture to pieces. But few will dare incur that responsibility because you spoil the piece."

This cultivator of the artistic sense talks to his friends of one of the best-known Paris collectors, who bought at an enormous price an "eighteenth century" writing desk:

"He purchased with a written guarantee from a respectable dealer, who was in good faith. Well, this table comes from my own workroom, only if I told the owner he probably would not believe me."

A dealer who lives not far from the church of the Madeline in Paris keeps the choicest "fakes" in his bedroom. He never shows his private collection, as he calls it, until the wealthy amateur tearfully begs to see it. The gem of the collection is the dealer's own bed in Louis XVI style.

He has sold his bed five or six times, but still sleeps well, I suppose because he "lies so easy," like a most honorable Frenchman.

At this moment, eighteenth-century engravings, including colored prints, are counterfeited on a vast scale.

Jewelry is made to look old by steeping in sulphuric acid for silver, or *aqua regia* for gold. The surface is worn with ground brick. The stones are then inserted and the whole is greased with tallow and rubbed in white soot.

Greek and Roman jewels, Renaissance enamels, Episcopal rings, and Benvenuto Cellini plate are "made in Germany."

Vienna is specialized in counterfeiting sixteenth-century enamels.

Abbeville and Armiens make flint arrow-tops and hatchets for museums of geology.

Old pewters are manufactured at Roden. Etruscan pottery comes from Leeds.

In Holland, I met a student who was in demand as he could forge any of the old masters' signatures on oil paintings.

FAMOUS SWINDLES

For years it has been a constant wonder to me how barefaced swindling operations are carried on in almost open defiance of the laws of the land. There are a thousand-and-one-get-rich quick schemes that each find their victims; it is needless to say that they bring wealth only to the promoter. There are more ways of swindling than with loaded dice and gold bricks.

Stock is sold in mining property where neither gold or silver ever existed, and the only metal about the proposition is the brazen cheek of the organizer of the company. Great promises of dividends are made, which are sometimes even paid out of the money received from the sale of the stock. Oil wells, gold mines, silver mines, and copper mines are exploited in this way to the great profit of the exploiter. A species of swindle that has been perpetrated times without number all over this country is the old gold-brick game. It does seem as though this had been exposed so frequently that the most ignorant country man would know enough to keep away from any one who offers to sell an ingot or "brick" of pure gold at a sacrifice; but still there are pigeons to be plucked. The usual method is to meet a likely person and with great show of secrecy unfold the story of the poor Mexican miner who has a lump of pure gold valued at $5,000, which he will sell for $500 down! The pigeon comes fluttering, drawn by the tempting bait; meets the miner, sees the glittering brick, handles it, even tests it with acid, and, finally, is induced to put down his good money. With great show of secrecy and caution the brick is handed over and the victim departs only to learn later that "all is not gold that glitters" and that he is out his $500!

Much ingenuity is exercised in fixing up the "brick" so it will stand inspection. Sometimes even wedges of good gold are inserted in the cheap metal, and the operator saws or files into this wedge to take out gold for the victim to test. In these enlightened days, I do not need to tell you that all such stories, no matter how plausible, should be questioned and rejected at once.

The greengoods swindle is an elaborate game which begins with some very adroit correspondence in which the writer claims to be in possession of some old and discarded steel plates used in printing United States money, and for that reason he is able to produce actual greenbacks which will pass anywhere. The letter usually begins something like this:

> *Dear Sir:* — I am in possession of a good thing and with your confidential and friendly cooperation I can make you independently rich and at the same time better my own condition. . . . You will see that my goods are not what the law can class as real counterfeits, inasmuch as they are printed from genuine plates and can easily be passed in your section of the country.

The letter goes on to explain the necessity of a personal interview, offers to guarantee travelling expenses, and quotes prices usually as follows: $300 real money buys $3,000; $1,000 buys $30,000, etc. The pigeon is given a password and number with which he must sign all telegrams. Finally, not to go into too many details, the green goods operator and the victim meet with great secrecy— a package of real money is produced for inspection, the purchase money is paid over, and the package which has been deftly exchanged for another package containing worthless paper is given to the purchaser, who departs to learn his loss as soon as he opens his bundle.

Of course, there is no redress possible. The whole

game is a swindle. Never but once to the best of my knowledge have actual original plates been stolen from the government, and that was when Langdon W. Moore was able to use his influence with a gang of counterfeiters and secure the return of the 5–20 bond plate in the early 80s as described in Chapter XV of his autobiography. Even if the plates were stolen as the green goods man pretends, the bills printed from them by unauthorized persons would be counterfeit in the eyes of the law.

Keep just as far away from any such scheme as you can.

THE FAIR CRIMINAL

There have arisen in every country, and in every age, celebrated women criminals whose daring deeds have become part of history.

From Lucrezia Borgia of the fifteenth century to Cassie Chadwick of the present day, the list is a long one, and yet police officials and prosecuting officers will no doubt agree with me, when I say that there are vastly fewer women criminals than men who lead dishonest lives.

The truth seems to be that when lovely woman stoops to crime, she usually goes to the greatest lengths of iniquity, and the comparatively few women who have perpetrated great crimes are made more conspicuous and more talked about by reason of their sex. In the United States, authorities claim that only one-tenth of persons accused of crime are women; while in France, Statistician Tarde declares that one-sixth is the usual proportion. Women criminals are certain to end their careers in wretchedness, if not in prison. Mothers of wayward girls are often much to blame for the beginning of careers of vice. A good home is the best protection, and upon every fair reader I urge the wisdom not only of choosing for herself the better way, but of safeguarding her sisters everywhere.

"Sophie" Lyons may be taken as a typical case of a born woman criminal. She came of a race of criminals. Her grandfather was a noted burglar in England, her father and mother, who came to America before she was born, both had a criminal record. She was taught to steal as soon as she could walk, and at twelve was arrested for shoplifting. At sixteen she was married to Maury Harris, a pickpocket, but her husband was sentenced to two years in State prison before the honeymoon was over. Later she married "Ned" Lyons, the noted burglar, and became one of the most expert female pickpockets in the country.

"Sophie" Lyons was a beautiful girl with brilliant dark eyes, abundant auburn hair, and a fascinating manner. At the county fairs she would make the acquaintance of men of wealth, and deftly relieve them of their watch or roll of banknotes, while they were fascinated with her blandishments. If caught, she was a consummate actress, and could counterfeit every shade of emotion. Real tears of injured innocence would flow from her beautiful eyes. Lyons pulled off a big coup about two years after their marriage, bought a villa on Long Island with the proceeds, and, though a professional burglar himself, tried to keep his wife from stealing. The taint was too strong, however; she picked pockets for the love of it. Eventually, both husband and wife were sentenced to Sing Sing Prison, from which they made a sensational escape and got away to Paris. In France, under the name of Madame d' Varney, she continued her brilliant career of crime. Sophie Lyons is supposed to be at large at the present time—somewhere in America. She has one son serving a term in State prison, and two daughters who are being carefully educated in Germany, kept as far as possible in ignorance of their mother's actual character.

The career of Cassie Chadwick, the "Duchess of Diamonds" is of more recent date. She is a woman of about fifty years of age, and has neither great physical beauty nor great personal charm, yet she must have had wonderful powers of persuasion, for she victimized such men as Andrew Carnegie, and made Banker Ira Reynolds believe she was an illegitimate child of the Scotch millionaire. With him she deposited a bundle of securities alleged to be worth $5,000,000 and a note for half a million dollars bearing Carnegie's signature. A signed paper from Reynolds attesting the fact that he held $5,000,000 worth of securities in trust for her became her stock in trade, and she fleeced bankers and business men to the tune of one million dollars in money, and $150,000 worth of jewels in four years. In March, 1905, she was convicted, and is now serving a ten-year sentence in the Ohio State penitentiary. Thanksgiving, 1905, during my engagement at Keith's Theatre, I gave a performance for the prisoners in the county jail in Cleveland, and Mrs. Chadwick was to be entertained in her cell; but fifteen minutes before I was to show her a few conjuring tricks, she changed her mood, gave the jailer an argument, and refused to allow any one near her cell.

Of the army of women shoplifters, petty thieves, stool-pigeons for confidence men, etc., little need be said. Shoplifting seems to be the most common crime. Many women steal for mere wantonness, having no need of the articles or money. Kleptomania is a polite word for this offense, and, doubtless, there are cases of mental disorder and moral degeneracy which take this form.

The time-worn badger game, as it is called, is still frequently employed to fleece men. The confidence woman gets acquainted with some man of means, preferably a married man of family, and invites him to call at her apartments. She carries on her part of the flirtation to *"perfection"* till suddenly the doorbell rings, and in apparent fright she exclaims: "There comes my husband. He is furiously jealous and will kill you!"

The fictitious husband rushes in, a scene takes place, and the "husband" threatens to shoot or call in the police. Eventually, the matter is settled by the victim giving up a large sum of money rather than face a scandal. This is only one form of blackmail resorted to, to extort money, as the victim is often threatened with public exposé, etc. Pirates in petticoats frequently ply their trade on ocean and lake steamers. They are well dressed and ingratiate themselves with the passengers of both sexes, watching their opportunity to steal jewelry, or practise their threadbare confidence games.

A woman named Grace Mordaunt cleared many thousands of dollars in New York by occasionally advertising the following personal in the *Herald*: "Young widow, financially embarrassed wishes loan of $100 on a diamond ring worth twice as much. Address Box."

Miss Mordaunt was beautiful and fascinating. She

would produce a genuine diamond ring, and go with her victim to a jeweler to have it priced. At his office she would receive her money, and ask him with tears not to wear or show her ring for a few days, but lock it up in his safe. She then takes the ring, wraps it up in tissue paper, puts it in an envelope, and hands it sealed to the victim, and leaves, promising to repay the money with interest in a few days. She never returns, and at length the victim opens the envelope to find a brass ring with a glass diamond worth about 25 cents.

While in Austria some years ago, I heard of a most remarkable adventuress who went under the name of Madame Clarice B. Her particular form of swindle was to get acquainted with young men of good family and wealth, and entangle them in her meshes, and get declarations of marriage from them. She would get all she could out of her poor dupe, and then notify the family of the "engagement." The young man's parents would then be forced to buy her off with a large sum of money, when she would go to pastures new. But Madame Clarice met her Waterloo in Vienna. There she met an American student upon whom she worked her wiles even to the extent of going through a marriage ceremony with him. After a time she left him and went to Paris, but the adventuress who had broken so many hearts found her own touched at last. She was actually in love with her student husband whose face haunted her dreams. After a few days she returned to Vienna, sought him out, and confessed all, but threw herself on his mercy and love. The denouement, unusual in such cases, was that the couple were actually married, and today are living happily on the continent.

Many, many more incidents might be related of the

clever work of the fascinating woman criminal, but these should be sufficient to warn the unwary against trusting either their honor or their pocketbook to an unknown woman, no matter how beautiful.

THE BRACE GAME

Of all classes of criminals the professional gambler has probably played the most conspicuous part in fiction and melodrama. We all know the stage gambler, while the penny dreadful novels and storybooks are too often filled with descriptions of this kind of crime. The gambler of the stage and in the novel is but an exaggerated portrait of this type.

Gambling is the playing for money of games depending solely on chance, like roulette; or games of skill and chance like poker and other card games or billiards and the like. A gentleman may have the moral right to back his own opinion in a wager with money, and with true sportsman instinct stand success or defeat. Even a small stake at cards is dangerous, for it cultivates the habit of gambling, which may soon become a passion.

Gambling in itself is bad enough even when the game is square; but your professional gambler never plays the game that way. He is an expert with cards. His seemingly innocent shuffle of the pack gives him a full knowledge of where every card is located. He deals you a hand good enough to induce you to make dangerously high bets, but not high enough to win. He lures his victim by small winnings to destruction in the end. He uses cards so cleverly marked on the back that he can read the values of your hand as well as if he were looking over your shoulder, and govern his play accordingly. In faro and roulette he uses mechanical devices for controlling absolutely the winning numbers, and so cheats his victim from beginning to end. When a gambler employs a fraudulent deck of cards or a cheating roulette wheel or faro-box it is called a "brace" game.

No novice can go up against a brace game with any hope of winning; he must lose. Even if the game were on the square the victim will invariably lose in the long run, for the percentage of chance is against him.

If the exposures, which I feel at liberty to make in this chapter, may warn the unwary and deter the youth of this land from the fascinations of the green cloth, I shall feel that my efforts have not been in vain.

Marked cards employed by gamblers are specially engraved packs of cards in which the usual decoration design of scrolls and flowers on the back, instead of being exactly identical on the fifty-two cards, is varied slightly for each of the high cards. This would not be noticed and cannot be detected without close examination, but it renders the back of the cards as legible to the gambler as the face. The turn of a leaf in the scroll work may mean that that card is the ace of diamonds, while a slightly different turn may mean the ace of hearts and so on.

With such a pack of cards the gambler has the poor dupe at his mercy. "Long cards" and strippers, as they are called, are special packs in which the high cards are slightly different in shape and width, enabling the gambler, for instance, with a single motion to take three of the aces out of a pack...

One of the most malicious little devices I have ever run across is sometimes called a vest-pock roulette wheel. It would seem that this must be square and that the player would have even a greater chance to win than on an ordinary wheel because there is only one zero. As a matter of fact, however, it is a fraud pure and simple, as the mechanism is so arranged that the pointer will stop on zero three times when it will stop on any other number once! So beware of the man with a little Monte Carlo in his pocket.

Among other things used by professional gamblers to cheat with are loaded dice which may be bought or made to order; adhesive palming cloth for palming cards, chips, dice, etc.; adhesive dice which almost defy detection; shaped dice which are not exact cubes; "brace" dice boxes; magnifying mirrors set in rings; shading boxes made to sew on inside of coat and used to shade or mark cards while the game is in progress; marked decks of cards, ring hold outs, bouncers for roulette wheels, cement for plugging dice, silver amalgam for loading dice, "brace" faro boxes, etc., etc. With such an equipment, united with years of experience and skill, what chance has any law-abiding citizen against the professional gambler? The reader does not need my secret of escaping from handcuffs to shake off the shackles of this alluring siren gambling.

CHEATING UNCLE SAM

Under this heading I shall group such crimes as counterfeiting and the kindred crimes of forgery and raising

notes, as well as smuggling. It is a serious matter to get
into trouble with the Federal government. The criminal
is pursued relentlessly, and the sentence when convic-
tion follows the almost certain arrest is always a heavy
one. For these reasons such crimes are usually attempted
only by the boldest and most skilful criminals or by those
whose positions of trust in government employ afford
them special opportunities.

The three great crimes against any government (aside,
of course, from actual treason) are counterfeiting its
money, either gold, silver, or bills; evading its custom laws,
or smuggling. Counterfeiting, which offers enormous
rewards if successful, is frequently attempted—indeed,
scarcely a month passes that does not see the appearance
of some new and dangerous counterfeit of some United
States bill. Notice is at once sent to all the banks by the
authorities and often published in the newspapers, so
that the public at large may be warned against the spuri-
ous bill in circulation.

Many years ago, when the art of engraving and plate
making was in its infancy, the paper money in circulation
was much more crude than today. Then it was comparatively easy for the counterfeiter to engrave just as good a
bill as the government could produce; but now the matter
is much more difficult, owing to the delicate and intri-
cate work of the lathe and tool work and the special fibre
paper upon which it is printed. The conditions of caution surrounding the government printing works make
it almost impossible for an original plate to be stolen.
The paper is made especially for this purpose and under
strictest government supervision. In designing, letter-
ing, and engraving the bills only artists of the foremost

professional standing are employed. Every banknote or greenback is truly a work of art, so that an exact counterfeit—one that will deceive even an ordinary business man accustomed to handle money—is each year more and more difficult to produce...

Genuine gold and silver coins are often tampered with. These schemes are known as "sweating," "plugging," and "filling." For instance, a hundred gold ten-dollar pieces subject to an acid bath would lose perhaps $35 or $40 worth of their gold and remain unchanged in appearance. The coins are put in circulation again, and the gold which has been "sweated" off of them is easily extracted from the acid bath and sold. Coins are also robbed of precious metal by drilling a hole, the cavity being filled with an alloy and the filling covered with a light gold wash. Filling a coin is sawing it through the edge in two parts, scraping out the gold, and putting the two parts together again filled with some baser metal. Thomas Ballard was the first counterfeiter to successfully reproduce government fibre paper, which he did in 1870. The next year he and his gang were captured, but escaped from jail and found a hiding-place from which they continued to issue dangerous counterfeits. In 1873 his counterfeit $500 treasury note alarmed banks and government officials. Ballard was finally captured in his lair in Buffalo just as he was about to produce a counterfeit $5 bill of a Canadian bank. This bill, he boasted, was to have corrupted all Canada.

John Peter McCartney was the counterfeiter who successfully removed all the ink from genuine $1 bills so that he could secure government paper on which to print counterfeit bills of much higher denomination. He made a fortune, so it is said, but was brought to book at last.

To a counterfeiter named "One-eyed Thompson" is given the credit of being the first to transform bills of small denomination to larger by cutting and pasting. He also had an ingenious trick of cutting up $10 or $100 bills into strips and making eleven counterfeit bills of the same denomination.

A German by the name of Charles Ulrich won the distinction of having produced the most dangerous Bank of England notes ever made.

Langdon W. Moore, one time expert bank robber, forger, and counterfeiter, who has now reformed and is leading an honest life, has written an interesting autobiography in which he tells of his own experience in raising notes, counterfeiting, and getting the counterfeits in circulation. At one time another gang of counterfeiters declared war on him. He sent a spy into the enemy's camp, learned where they were going to put out their next batch of "queer," and then proceeded to carry out a plan for outwitting them.

Postage stamp counterfeits are common enough, but mostly practised to impose on the collectors of rare stamps: for instance, a certain issue of Hawaiian stamps are very valuable as there are not supposed to be more than half a dozen or so in existence, and when one is found it sells for thousands of dollars. One of the most daring stamp counterfeiters "planted" about twenty forgeries of this rare stamp into collections of wealthy philatelists and realized many thousands of dollars.

Another daring gang introduced a beautifully engraved stamp into Paris by posing as the "King of Sodang" and suite—Sodang being an island that existed solely in the imagination of the clever swindler. A stamp dealer was the principal victim and paid the "king" a large sum of money for a number of the stamps of this fictitious kingdom.

Speaking of stamps recalls a method of secret writing which defied detection. The plan was to put a fake letter inside the envelope, but to write the real message in microscopic characters in the upper right-hand corner, and over this paste the stamp. The correspondent, who was, of course, in the secret, would simply soak off the stamp.

This trick is often made use of by convicts who wish to send a secret message to their friends on the outside.

Cancelled postage stamps are frequently washed and sold or used again. I have in my possession a receipt given me by a Russian convict which will do this perfectly, removing every trace of the cancellation mark, but leaving the stamp perfect. Such a secret is too dangerous, however, for general publication.

On the continent I have known of a clever dodge being practised which reaches the same result. Before the letter is mailed the stamp is covered with a transparent paste. When the letter is received the correspondent can simply wash off the stamp with water, and, of course, the cancellation marks with it. The penalty for this crime is so severe, and the reward so small, that not even hardened criminals are willing to risk the attempt.

A clever gang of smugglers adopted this ruse in order to get their trunks through the custom-house free. They had counterfeit labels made, such as an inspector places upon a trunk. Passing among the trunks where the inspectors were at work they would slyly poke the "inspected" label on all their own trunks. Each official seeing the labels would suppose some other official had actually inspected the trunks and so would pass on to others.

Instances might be multiplied, but all goes to show that dishonesty, whether to your fellowmen or to the government, is the worst of all policies in the end.

HUMBUGS

A humbug or a hoax is often comparatively harmless in its nature—more in the way of a high practical joke upon the public. Long ago P. T. Barnum, the great American showman, declared: "The American people want to be humbugged." I believe he was right and certainly his great success in the show business would seem to point to the same conclusion. In my own particular work I find there is so much that is marvellous and wonderful that can be accomplished by perfectly natural means that I have no need to find recourse to humbugging the public. In my case, at least, truth is stranger than fiction.

At the present day a firm in New York makes a business of manufacturing fakes like double-bodied babies, mermaids, and fake mummies. Dr. L.D. Weiss, of New York, discovered that he could detect a fake mummy from an original by placing it under his X-Ray machine.

Another clever hoax which created much amusement at the time was contrived by some English students years ago and perpetrated at a county fair. On a vacant lot near the fair a large tent was erected and a huge placard announced that "The Great Wusser" was on exhibition within—admission free! It was supposed that some payment or purchase would be required inside, but it was not so. The crowd, eager for free amusement, was formed into a long "queue," and the people—admitted only one at a time—were escorted through a maze of hurdles into a darkened compartment of the tent before a curtain. There they were entreated not to irritate or disturb the "animal" in any way, and the curtain went up, disclosing a sorry and spavined looking donkey. "This is the great Wusser," explained the showman. And when the bewildered spectator asked what it meant, he was told that, "though you may have seen as bad a donkey, you certainly never saw a wusser!" Then, when the victim of the hoax became indignant, he was besought to "keep it quiet" and take his revenge by allowing the remainder of the crowd to be hoaxed. This request showed a deep knowledge of human nature, for the victim always complied, and many went among the crowd and spread the most astonishing accounts of the "Great Wusser," and waited to see their comrades taken in. Eventually, however, rioting arose, and the jesters, being arrested for creating a disturbance, had to pay over $100 in fines and damages.

But humbugs are not all so harmless. An adroit rascal was caught not long ago in London who was posing as an American bishop. He was certainly a great humbug, for he looked the part of the "bishop" to perfection. It seems that he called in his carriage, mind you, at a well-known jewelers and asked to see some bracelets, mentioning that he was returning to America and wished to take a present to his wife. "Nothing very expensive," he said—"I could not afford that—but something about seventy or eighty pounds." Eventually, he agreed to take a bracelet that cost one hundred pounds. He said he would pay for it with a hundred pound note which he had with him. It was the only money he had with him at the moment, but he would wait while they sent it to the bank to ascertain that it was all right. He should really prefer doing this. They sent it to the bank and received answer that it was perfectly correct.

Having paid for his bracelet the bishop took it and was just about to step into his carriage when a policeman tapped him on the shoulder, and said, "Hellow Jim! You're up to your old tricks again, are you? You just come along with me," and he took him back into the shop.

The jeweler said there was some mistake, that the gentleman was an American bishop, that he had bought a bracelet, and paid for it with an excellent note.

"Just let me look at the note, will you?" said the policeman. He looked at it, and said, "yes, it's just as I thought. This note is one of a particularly clever batch of forgeries which are very difficult to detect, and the man is no more a bishop than you are. We will go off to the police station at once. I will take the note and go on with the prisoner in advance, and you must send your salesman to me and meet us and bear witness." So the policeman took the bishop and the bracelet and the note, but when the jeweler's man reached the police station they had not arrived, and they have never been heard of since!

HOUDINI

How does he do it? That is the usual question I hear asked about my work in the theater. No, dear reader, it is not my purpose to tell you *how* I open locks, *how* I escape from a prison cell into which I have been locked, having previously been stripped naked and manacled with heavy irons. I do not intend to tell you in this book *how* I escape from the trunk or the tightly corded and nailed-up box in which I have been confined, or *how* I unlock any regulation handcuff that can be produced—not yet.

Some day I may tell all this, and then you will know. At present, I prefer that all who see me should draw their own conclusions. But exactly how I accomplish these things I shall still leave you to guess, gentle reader. I should not want you to go into the show business. It's a hard life, "so they say."

"Have you ever been stuck at it?" I think I hear you ask. Not yet. I have had some pretty close calls, but have always pulled through somehow. The nearest I ever came to giving in was during my engagement at Blackbourne, England. There I offered a prize to the man who could fasten me in such a way that I could not escape. One man accepted my challenge. He was an instructor in athletics, and was out for blood. He evidently looked upon my challenge as a personal affront to him. At any rate, he started in to shackle me.

He first handcuffed my hands in front, then locked elbow irons, the chain of which went behind my back. Then he handcuffed my legs, and after this bent me backward and chained my back and feet together. I had to kneel down. Every chain and handcuff was fitted to the limit. I started in, but at the end of an hour I suffered so under the strain that I asked to be let out. My back was aching, my circulation was stopped in my wrists, and my arms became paralyzed. My opponent's only reply was, "This is a bet. Cry quits or keep on."

The Music Hall where I was playing was packed, and while watching me became fairly wild. I kept on, but I was only about half conscious. Every joint in my body was aching, and I had but little use of my arms. I asked as a favor that he free my hands long enough for the circular tion to start again, but he only laughed and exclaimed, "This is no love affair, this is a contest. Say you are defeated and I'll release you."

I gritted my teeth and went at it once more. For two hours and a half I exerted myself, fighting for my professional good name. In the meanwhile, the audience was cheering itself hoarse. Some cried "Give it up," and others, "Keep on, you'll do it." I don't believe any such scene was ever acted in a theater. The house was crazy with excitement, and I was covered with blood brought on by my exertion to release myself and chaffing irons. But I did it. I got free of every chain and handcuff. Then they had to carry me off the stage, and I suffered from the effects for months afterwards.

As for the prison cell, I have never been locked in one I could not open. I have had the honor of making my escape from securely locked cells in jails, prisons, and police stations in almost every large city in the world, and under the most rigid conditions. The chiefs of police, the wardens, the jailers, the detectives, and citizens who have been present at these tests know that they are real and actual. Perhaps the most historic American feat that gained for me the most notoriety was my escape January, 1906, from Cell 2, Murderers' Row, in the United States Jail at Washington, D. C.; from the very cell in which Guiteau, the assassin of President Garfield, was confined until he was led forth to be hanged. Since my return from abroad, October, 1905, I have escaped after being locked up in a nude state from cells in New York City, Brooklyn, Detroit, Rochester, Buffalo, Washington, Baltimore, Philadelphia, Providence, and City Tombs in Boston and Lowell. In all cases I submitted to a close search, being stark naked and heavily manacled into the cell, which was also thoroughly searched.

I am an American by birth, born in Appleton, Wis., USA, on April 6, 1873. To my lot have fallen more experiences, more strange adventures, more ups, and downs, in my thirty-three years of life than to most men.

When about nine years of age my mother, to whom I am greatly attached, apprenticed me to a mechanic to learn that trade; but, after an uneventful term with the tools of the trade, I resolved to see the world with my own eager eyes. So I ran away from home, and in this way made an early acquaintance with the corrugated side of life.

I joined a small circus, and soon learned to conduct the Punch and Judy show, to do a ventriloquial act, and to play town clown on the bars—"gol darn it." I also doubled in brass—that is, I beat the cymbals. I here gained the experiences that possibly ripened me into the world's Handcuff King and Prison Breaker—a title which I have justly earned.

But there was a time when I was not recognized as I am now. Those were the days of small things. That was in the middle West. After that, London and an engagement at the Alhambra. After that, everywhere on the continent and all over America. I have not yet been to Australia. I do not wish to be so far away from my mother.

While touring Germany I brought suit against the police and a newspaper because they said my act was not genuine. I won the case—to have lost it would have meant ruin.

Again, in Russia, I was bound by the officials of the spy police and locked in a Siberian transport cell. Had I failed to escape, I would have been compelled to journey to Siberia, as the key that locks these cells does not open them. The governor-general in Siberia has the only key to open them. I was out in twenty minutes.

If there were more room in this book I would like to tell you of the many places in which I have played, both in America and Europe. I have many certificates from police officials. I was almost too busy to write this book, although I have been collecting the material for a long time. But now I am pleased it is written, and trust it may please you. I believe that the reading of this book will so familiarize the public with the methods of the criminal classes that it will enable law-abiding citizens to protect themselves from the snares of the evil-doer.

I hope it will warn you away from crime and all evil-doing. It may tell the "Right Way to Do Wrong," but, as I said in the beginning, all I have to say is "Don't."

THE NEVERSINK LIBRARY

THE NEVERSINK LIBRARY